BELIEVE IT!
QUICK AND EASY MEAL SOLUTIONS

Cooking Club of America™

Meredith® Books
Des Moines, Iowa

Believe It! Quick and Easy Meal Solutions
Editors: Jessica Saari, Alrica Goldstein
Contributing Graphic Designers: Renee E. McAtee, Angie Hoogensen
Copy Chief: Doug Kouma
Copy Editor: Kevin Cox
Publishing Operations Manager: Karen Schirm
Senior Editor, Asset and Information Management: Phillip Morgan
Edit and Design Production Coordinator: Mary Lee Gavin
Editorial Assistant: Sheri Cord
Book Production Manager: Mark Weaver
Imaging Center Operator: Mitchell Barlow
Photographers: Jason Donnelly, Scott Little, Blaine Moats, Jay Wilde
Contributing Proofreaders: Karen Fraley, Stacie Gaylor, Donna Segal
Contributing Indexer: Elizabeth T. Parson
Test Kitchen Director: Lynn Blanchard
Test Kitchen Product Supervisor: Colleen Weeden
Test Kitchen Culinary Specialists: Marilyn Cornelius, Juliana Hale, Maryellyn Krantz, Jill Moberly, Colleen Weeden, Lori Wilson
Test Kitchen Nutrition Specialists: Elizabeth Burt, R.D., L.D.; Laura Marzen, R.D., L.D.

Meredith® Books
Editorial Director: John Riha
Deputy Editor: Jennifer Darling
Managing Editor: Kathleen Armentrout
Brand Manager: Janell Pittman
Group Editor: Jan Miller

Director, Marketing and Publicity: Amy Nichols
Executive Director, Sales: Ken Zagor
Director, Operations: George A. Susral
Director, Production: Douglas M. Johnston
Business Director: Janice Croat

Vice President and General Manager, SIM: Jeff Myers

Better Homes and Gardens® Magazine
Editor in Chief: Gayle Goodson Butler
Deputy Editor, Food and Entertaining: Nancy Hopkins

Meredith Publishing Group
President: Jack Griffin
Executive Vice President: Doug Olson

Meredith Corporation
Chairman of the Board: William T. Kerr
President and Chief Executive Officer: Stephen M. Lacy

In Memoriam: E. T. Meredith III (1933–2003)

First Edition.

Printed in the United States of America.
ISBN: 978-1-58159-405-8

This edition published by the Cooking Club of America by arrangement with Meredith Publishing.

All of us at Meredith® Books are dedicated to providing you with the information and ideas you need to create delicious foods. We welcome your comments and suggestions.
Write to us at: Meredith Books, Cookbook Editorial Department, 1716 Locust St., Des Moines, IA 50309-3023.

Pictured on front cover: Rosemary Chicken with Vegetables, page 73

Dinner is back!

Who has time to cook??? Between Monday-night soccer practice and Wednesday-night music lessons, family life can be very hectic—sometimes even a little frantic! And after working all day, driving the kids around town, and running all your errands, finding the time to whip together a home-cooked meal may seem like a daunting task. But stop . . . and take a deep breath.

Meals at home are possible. No matter how much or how little time you have to put good food on the table for yourself and your family, there's a recipe in here for you. Whether it's 10 minutes or 30 minutes until suppertime, you can find a soup, salad, sandwich, or entree that quiets your family's I'm-hungry-right-now demands. There are also comforting favorites that you can load into the slow cooker in the morning and not think about again until you get home at night. For lunch? Bag it up and bring it to work or school with these quick-fix sandwiches and salads.

Believe It! Quick and Easy Meal Solutions was created just for you—the time-crunched grown-ups who are juggling everything but also know the importance of home-cooked meals for themselves and their families. For that reason, these recipes were designed to be not only irresistible but also easy to prepare and fast to the table. So go ahead—enjoy food again!

brown baggin' it

how to pack a safe to-go lunch

Ever worry about the time that passes between making a sack lunch and eating it? Follow these tips to keep your noontime meal free of foodborne bacteria.

Let's be honest: Most sack lunches sit awhile before they're eaten. The best way to keep bacteria from growing is to remember these rules from the Partnership for Food Safety Education: Clean, separate, cook, and chill. Clean your hands, work surface, and food. Separate produce from meat products, using separate cutting boards for each. Keep cooked foods hot, and keep cold foods chilled. Below are three quick ways to protect you and your kids from foodborne illnesses.

* Wash your hands with warm, soapy water for 20 seconds before and after handling food or eating. Teach your kids to do the same. Wash all fruits and vegetables before packing them in a sack lunch.

* Buy a lunch bag that's insulated. Use an insulated bottle for hot food, and use an ice pack or freezer gel pack for cold food. Throw away any perishable items not eaten at lunch. This includes sandwiches made with beef, tuna, turkey, chicken, egg, or ham, as well as mayonnaise-based salad spreads and dressings.

* Store lunches in the refrigerator—not on the kitchen counter—if you pack them the night before. Throw away cold foods left unrefrigerated for more than two hours. Check to make sure your refrigerator is 40°F or below at all times.

Gross! The American Dietetic Association found **nearly 60 percent of kids don't wash their hands** before eating lunch. Help them out by packing hand sanitizer in their lunch bag for quick cleaning.

Inside-Out Turkey Tempters

Start to Finish: 15 minutes

- **12** **thin slices cooked turkey breast**
- **2** **purchased soft breadsticks (6 to 8 inches long), halved lengthwise**
- **½** **cup flavored reduced-fat cream cheese (½ of an 8-ounce container)**
- **½** **cup packaged fresh julienned carrots**
- **4** **bread-and-butter or dill pickle spears**
- **Leaf lettuce (optional)**

1. Overlap 3 turkey slices so meat is the same length as breadstick halves. Spread turkey meat with 2 tablespoons of the cream cheese. Place 2 tablespoons of the carrots, one pickle spear, and one breadstick half on edge of turkey. Roll up so meat is wrapped around breadstick. If desired, roll one or two lettuce leaves around outside of sandwich. Repeat with remaining ingredients. Makes 4 servings.
2. For individual lunches, wrap rolls; chill.

Per serving: 194 cal., 5 g fat (3 g sat. fat), 49 mg chol., 395 mg sodium, 19 g carbo., 1 g fiber, 18 g pro.

Crunchy PB&A Wraps

Start to Finish: 5 minutes

- **⅓** **cup peanut butter**
- **4** **7- to 8-inch flour tortillas**
- **1** **cup chopped apple**
- **¼** **cup low-fat granola**

1. Spread peanut butter over each tortilla. Sprinkle evenly with apple and granola. Tightly roll up tortillas. Cut in half.
2. For individual lunches, wrap tortillas and chill. Makes 4 servings.

Per serving: 254 cal., 14 g fat (3 g sat. fat), 0 mg chol., 234 mg sodium, 28 g carbo., 3 g fiber, 8 g pro.

Tomato-Turkey Wraps

Prep: 20 minutes

- 1 **7-ounce container prepared hummus (plain or desired flavor)**
- 3 **9- to 10-inch tomato-basil-flavor flour tortillas or plain flour tortillas**
- 8 **ounces thinly sliced, cooked peppered turkey breast**
- 6 **romaine lettuce leaves, ribs removed**
- 3 **small tomatoes, thinly sliced**
- 3 **thin slices red onion, separated into rings**

1. Spread hummus evenly over tortillas. Layer turkey breast, romaine, tomatoes, and red onion on top of hummus. Roll up each tortilla into a spiral. Cut each tortilla in half. Wrap each half with plastic wrap. Serve immediately or chill for up to 4 hours.* Makes 6 wraps.

***Tip:** Wrapping and chilling rolled tortillas helps them keep their shape when unwrapped, making them easier to eat.

Per wrap: 221 cal., 6 g fat (1 g sat. fat), 16 mg chol., 926 mg sodium, 29 g carbo., 3 g fiber, 14 g pro.

GREAT SIDES FOR YOU

❊ Apple ❊ Pear ❊ Hard-cooked eggs ❊ Soy chips or baked chips ❊ 100-calorie snack packs of cookies ❊ Unsweetened iced tea or low-calorie soda ❊ Veggies

GREAT SIDES FOR KIDS

❊ Banana ❊ Grapes ❊ Unsweetened applesauce pack ❊ Small bag of pretzels ❊ Raisin boxes ❊ Reduced-calorie pudding snacks ❊ White or chocolate milk

Car-Hoppin' Chicken Cups

Start to Finish: 15 minutes

- ¼ **cup plain low-fat yogurt**
- ¼ **cup bottled reduced-fat ranch salad dressing**
- 1½ **cups chopped cooked chicken or turkey**
- ½ **cup chopped broccoli**
- ¼ **cup shredded carrot**
- ¼ **cup chopped pecans or walnuts (optional)**

1. In a small bowl, stir together the yogurt and salad dressing.

2. In a medium bowl, combine chicken, broccoli, carrot, and, if desired, nuts. Pour yogurt mixture over chicken mixture; toss to coat. Divide chicken mixture among 4 plastic cups. Cover and chill up to 24 hours. Makes 4 servings.

Per serving: 146 cal., 7 g fat (1 g sat. fat), 53 mg chol., 225 mg sodium, 4 g carbo., 0 g fiber, 16 g pro.

Ham & Pickle Wrap

This wrap actually improves after a short time in the refrigerator. The flavors blend and the tortilla softens as it sits.

Prep: 5 minutes

- **1 tablespoon bottled ranch salad dressing**
- **1 7- to 8-inch whole wheat or plain flour tortilla**
- **2 thin slices cooked ham (about 1½ ounces)**
- **1 to 2 thin lengthwise slices bread-and-butter pickles**

1. Spread salad dressing over tortilla. Top with ham and pickle. Roll up. Wrap in plastic wrap. If desired, chill for up to 6 hours. If desired, cut wrap into halves or thirds and secure with toothpicks. Makes 1 wrap.

Per serving: 284 cal., 13 g fat (3 g sat. fat), 29 mg chol., 1,103 mg sodium, 30 g carbo., 3 g fiber, 11 g pro.

Chicken & Hummus Wraps

These wraps are a good way to introduce new flavors to your kids. Look for hummus in the deli or health-food section of your local grocery store.

Prep: 15 minutes

- **1 7-ounce carton desired-flavor hummus or one 8-ounce tub cream cheese spread with garden vegetables**
- **4 10-inch flour tortillas**
- **⅓ cup plain low-fat yogurt or dairy sour cream**
- **1 6-ounce package refrigerated cooked chicken breast strips**
- **¾ cup coarsely chopped roma tomato (2 large)**
- **¾ cup thinly sliced cucumber**

1. Spread hummus evenly over tortillas; spread yogurt over top of hummus. Top with chicken, tomatoes, and cucumber. Roll tortillas up tightly. Makes 4 servings.

Per wrap: 288 cal., 9 g fat (2 g sat. fat), 31 mg chol., 713 mg sodium, 36 g carbo., 3 g fiber, 16 g pro.

Dizzy Sandwich Rolls

Pack rolls with fresh fruit (peeled orange, grapes, or banana) and a plastic storage bag with whole-grain chips.

Start to Finish: 15 minutes

- 2 tablespoons whipped cream cheese spread*
- 1 8- or 9-inch tortilla (any flavor)
- ¼ cup shredded carrot
- 1 tablespoon dried tart cherries or raisins
- 1 ounce thinly sliced cooked ham or turkey

1. Spread the cream cheese evenly over tortilla. Top with carrot and cherries. Top evenly with ham. Roll up; cut into quarters. Wrap tightly in plastic wrap. Makes 1 serving.

***Note:** If desired, substitute cream cheese spread with garden vegetables or with chives and onion for plain cream cheese.

Per serving: 334 cal., 11 g fat (5 g sat. fat), 2 mg chol., 796 mg sodium, 45 g carbo., 4 g fiber, 12 g pro.

Ham Focaccia Sandwich

Start to Finish: 10 minutes

- **1 individual Italian flatbread (focaccia) or ciabatta roll**
- **1 tablespoon bottled creamy garlic or ranch salad dressing**
- **1 romaine lettuce leaf**
- **1 slice leftover cooked ham or deli sliced cooked ham**
- **1 slice provolone cheese**
- **2 cherry tomatoes, thinly sliced**
- **1 tablespoon chopped roasted red sweet pepper**

1. Slice the bread in half horizontally. Spread salad dressing on the cut side of the bottom half. On the bottom half, layer romaine lettuce, ham, provolone, tomatoes, and sweet peppers. Cover with top half of roll; wrap. If desired, chill for up to 24 hours. Makes 1 sandwich.

Per serving: 461 cal., 19 g fat (7 g sat. fat), 45 mg chol., 1,235 mg sodium, 54 g carbo., 4 g fiber, 22 g pro.

Curried Pasta & Chicken Salad

Prep: 25 minutes

- 8 **ounces dried radiatore or rotini pasta (2 cups)**
- 2 **cups cubed cooked chicken**
- 1½ **cups seedless green grapes, halved**
- 1½ **cups cubed cantaloupe**
- ¾ **cup sliced celery**
- ½ **cup sliced green onion (4)**
- 1 **8-ounce carton plain low-fat yogurt**
- 3 **tablespoons mango chutney or orange marmalade**
- 1½ **teaspoons curry powder**
- ¼ **teaspoon salt**

1. Cook pasta according to package directions; drain. Rinse with cold water; drain again. In a large bowl, stir together pasta, chicken, grapes, cantaloupe, celery, and green onion.
2. In a small bowl, stir together yogurt, chutney, curry powder, and salt. Add to pasta mixture. Toss to coat; cover. If desired, chill up to 4 hours.
3. For lunches, spoon salad into 6 covered containers; chill. Makes 6 servings.

Per serving: 314 cal., 5 g fat (2 g sat. fat), 44 mg chol., 204 mg sodium, 46 g carbo., 3 g fiber, 21 g pro.

Ham & Cheese Calzones

Prep: 15 minutes **Bake:** 15 minutes
Cool: 30 minutes

- 1 **10-ounce package refrigerated pizza dough**
- ¼ **cup coarse-grain mustard**
- 6 **ounces sliced Swiss or provolone cheese**
- 1½ **cups cubed cooked ham (8 ounces)**
- ½ **teaspoon caraway seeds**

1. Preheat oven to 400°F. Line baking sheet with foil; lightly grease foil. Unroll dough. On a lightly floured surface, roll dough into a 15×10-inch rectangle. Cut into 4 equal rectangles.
2. Spread mustard over rectangles. Divide 3 ounces cheese among rectangles, placing slices on half of each. Top cheese with ham and caraway seeds. Top with remaining cheese. Brush edges of dough with water. Fold dough over filling to opposite edge, stretching if necessary. Seal edges.
3. Place calzones on baking sheet. Prick tops with a fork. Bake about 15 minutes or until golden. Cool on wire rack 30 minutes.
4. For individual lunches, wrap each sandwich and chill. Makes 4 servings.

Per serving: 421 cal., 21 g fat (10 g sat. fat), 72 mg chol., 1,390 mg sodium, 28 g carbo., 1 g fiber, 30 g pro.

Thai-Style Beef Salad

Make a roast beef and save the leftovers for this irresistible lunchtime salad.

Start to Finish: 15 minutes

- **2 tablespoons bottled Italian salad dressing**
- **2 to 3 teaspoons lime juice**
- **1½ teaspoons soy sauce**
- **1 teaspoon snipped fresh cilantro**
- **2 cups fresh spinach leaves or torn mixed salad greens**
- **¼ cup purchased shredded carrot**
- **½ cup shredded cooked roast beef**
- **1 tablespoon chopped peanuts**

1. For dressing, in a small container with a tight-fitting lid, combine dressing, lime juice, soy sauce, and cilantro; cover and shake well. If desired, chill for up to 24 hours.

2. In a container with a lid, combine spinach, carrot, beef, and peanuts. Cover. If desired, chill up to 24 hours.

3. To serve, shake dressing; add dressing to spinach mixture and toss to coat. Makes 1 serving.

Per serving: 328 cal., 22 g fat (5 g sat. fat), 56 mg chol., 1,095 mg sodium, 10 g carbo., 3 g fiber, 25 g pro.

Barbecue Beef Wrap

Do your kids turn up their noses at leftovers? Completely reinvent beef from last night with this delicious wrap.

Prep: 10 minutes

- ⅓ cup shredded cooked roast beef
- 1 7- to 8-inch flour tortilla
- 1 tablespoon bottled barbecue sauce
- 2 tablespoons shredded Monterey Jack cheese
- 2 tablespoons packaged shredded broccoli (broccoli slaw mix)

1. Arrange beef on tortilla. Drizzle with barbecue sauce and top with cheese and broccoli. Roll up. Wrap tightly in plastic wrap. If desired, chill up to 24 hours. Makes 1 serving.

Per serving: 280 cal., 13 g fat (6 g sat. fat), 57 mg chol., 367 mg sodium, 17 g carbo., 1 g fiber, 21 g pro.

Antipasto Tortellini Salad

Pack this salad in an individual-size airtight container and toss in the office fridge.

Prep: 25 minutes **Chill:** 2 hours

- **1 9-ounce package refrigerated cheese tortellini**
- **½ cup chopped bottled roasted red sweet pepper**
- **1 6-ounce jar marinated quartered artichoke hearts, drained**
- **¼ cup sliced pitted ripe olives**
- **1 ounce Genoa salami, cut into thin strips**
- **1 ounce provolone cheese, cubed**
- **¼ cup bottled vinaigrette salad dressing**

1. Cook tortellini according to package directions. Drain; place in a large bowl. Stir in sweet pepper, artichoke hearts, olives, salami, and cheese. Add dressing; toss to coat. Cover and refrigerate for 2 hours or overnight. Toss before serving. If necessary, toss with additional dressing to moisten. Makes 4 (1-cup) servings.

Per serving: 340 cal., 17 g fat (4 g sat. fat), 41 mg chol., 869 mg sodium, 36 g carbo., 1 g fiber, 14 g pro.

weeknight solutions

Savory Chicken with Pasta

If this dish is too grown-up for younger taste buds, pan-fry a couple extra seasoned chicken breasts and serve them with pasta—minus the sauce and veggies.

Start to Finish: 35 minutes

- **8 ounces angel hair pasta**
- **½ teaspoon dried thyme, crushed**
- **½ teaspoon salt**
- **¼ teaspoon ground black pepper**
- **2 boneless, skinless chicken breast halves, halved horizontally (about 12 ounces total)**
- **2 tablespoons olive oil**
- **8 ounces presliced mushrooms (3 cups)**
- **1 small red onion, halved and sliced (about 1 cup)**
- **1½ teaspoons bottled minced garlic**
- **1½ cups reduced-sodium chicken broth**
- **1 tablespoon all-purpose flour**
- **1 teaspoon Dijon-style mustard**
- **4 plum tomatoes, cut into thin wedges**
- **¼ cup chopped fresh flat-leaf (Italian) parsley**

1. Cook pasta according to package directions; drain well.

2. Meanwhile, in a small bowl, combine thyme, ¼ teaspoon of the salt, and the pepper. Sprinkle over both sides of each chicken breast. In a very large skillet, heat 1 tablespoon of the oil over medium-high heat. Add chicken to skillet. Reduce heat to medium and cook until golden and cooked through (170°F), about 6 minutes, turning once. Remove chicken from skillet; cover and keep warm.

3. Add remaining 1 tablespoon oil to the skillet. Heat over medium-high heat. Stir in mushrooms, onion, and garlic; cook, stirring occasionally, until onion is tender, about 5 minutes. Whisk together broth, flour, mustard, and remaining ¼ teaspoon salt; add to skillet. Cook and stir until slightly thickened and bubbly. Stir in tomato and parsley; heat through. Serve chicken and sauce with pasta. Makes 4 servings.

Per serving: 426 cal., 9 g fat (2 g sat. fat), 49 mg chol., 604 mg sodium, 53 g carbo., 4 g fiber, 31 g pro.

Challenge: I need a chicken meal that has more grown-up flavors.

Chicken & Pasta Primavera

Boiling the vegetables with the pasta is a good way to piggyback kitchen tasks to save time. Make sure the vegetables are thinly sliced so they cook through.

Start to Finish: 25 minutes

- 1 **9-ounce package refrigerated spinach or plain fettuccine**
- 1 **cup thinly sliced carrot (2 medium)**
- 1 **medium zucchini, halved lengthwise and thinly sliced (1¼ cups)**
- ¾ **cup frozen whole kernel corn**
- 12 **ounces deli-roasted chicken, cut into ½-inch strips (about 2½ cups)**
- 1½ **cups chicken broth**
- 4 **teaspoons cornstarch**
- 2 **teaspoons finely shredded lemon peel**
- 1 **teaspoon dried basil, crushed**
- ½ **cup dairy sour cream**
- 2 **tablespoons Dijon-style mustard**
- **Finely shredded Parmesan cheese**

1. Cook pasta according to package directions, adding carrots, zucchini, and corn to the water with pasta. Drain pasta and vegetables. Return all to saucepan; add chicken. (If the chicken has been refrigerated, place it in a colander. Pour the pasta, vegetables, and cooking liquid over chicken to warm it; drain well.)

2. Meanwhile, in a medium saucepan, stir together broth, cornstarch, lemon peel, and basil. Cook and stir over medium heat until thickened and bubbly. Cook and stir for 2 minutes more. Remove from heat. Stir in sour cream and mustard. Pour over pasta mixture; toss gently to coat. Sprinkle with cheese. Serve immediately. Makes 6 servings.

Per serving: 334 cal., 10 g fat (4 g sat. fat), 98 mg chol., 547 mg sodium, 34 g carbo., 3 g fiber, 27 g pro.

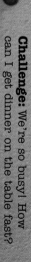

Challenge: We're so busy! How can I get dinner on the table fast?

Challenge: How can I get my toddler to eat vegetables?

Kids' Favorite Pasta & Chicken

Coated in flavored cream cheese and Parmesan, your kids will barely notice the veggies in this dish.

Start to Finish: 25 minutes

- 1 **12-ounce package frozen cooked breaded chicken nuggets**
- 8 **ounces dried wagon wheel pasta**
- 4 **cups sliced assorted vegetables (such as broccoli, summer squash, and sweet pepper)**
- ½ **of an 8-ounce tub cream cheese spread with chives and onion**
- ½ **cup milk**
- **Salt and ground black pepper**
- **Shredded Parmesan cheese**

1. Heat chicken nuggets according to package directions.

2. Meanwhile, in a Dutch oven, heat a large amount of lightly salted water to boiling. Add pasta; cook for 4 minutes. Add vegetables; cook for 5 minutes more or until pasta is tender. Drain and return to pan.

3. Add cream cheese spread to pasta mixture. Heat through. Add enough milk to thin to desired consistency. Season to taste with salt and pepper. Sprinkle with Parmesan before serving. Serve with baked chicken nuggets. Makes 4 servings.

Per serving: 643 cal., 27 g fat (12 g sat. fat), 81 mg chol., 811 mg sodium, 72 g carbo., 4 g fiber, 25 g pro.

Challenge: How do I encourage my children to try new flavors?

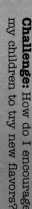

Ginger Chicken Stir-Fry

Here's a low-stress way to get finicky eaters to branch out with new tastes—such as ginger and stir-fry sauce. The flavors are mild enough for picky palates.

Start to Finish: 25 minutes

- **1 tablespoon cooking oil or peanut oil**
- **1 medium zucchini, thinly sliced**
- **1 medium carrot, thinly sliced**
- **1 small onion, thinly sliced**
- **1 small red sweet pepper, halved, seeded, and thinly sliced**
- **½ head small green cabbage, shredded**
- **12 ounces skinless, boneless chicken breast halves, cut into 1-inch pieces**
- **½ cup bottled stir-fry sauce**
- **½ teaspoon ground ginger**
- **Hot cooked rice**
- **Peanuts or cashews (optional)**

1. In a wok or extra-large skillet, heat oil over medium-high heat. Add half of the vegetables; stir-fry 2 minutes or until crisp-tender. Remove vegetables. Repeat with remaining vegetables; remove.

2. If necessary, add more oil to hot wok. Add chicken. Stir-fry for 3 to 5 minutes or until chicken is no longer pink. Push chicken from center of wok. Add sauce and ginger to center. Cook and stir until bubbly. Return cooked vegetables to wok. Cook and stir about 1 minute more or until vegetables are coated and heated through. Serve over hot cooked rice. If desired, sprinkle each serving with peanuts. Makes 6 servings.

Per serving, without rice: 130 cal., 3 g fat (1 g sat. fat), 34 mg chol., 540 mg sodium, 9 g carbo., 2 g fiber, 16 g pro.

Garlic Chicken

Homemade Asian-style food can be easier than you think to prepare. It's all in the sauce!

Prep: 20 minutes
Marinate: 30 minutes
Cook: 6 minutes

- 1 pound skinless, boneless chicken breasts
- 1 cup water
- 3 tablespoons reduced-sodium soy sauce
- 2 tablespoons chicken broth
- 1 tablespoon cornstarch
- 2 tablespoons cooking oil
- 10 green onions, bias-sliced
- 1 cup thinly sliced fresh mushrooms
- 12 cloves garlic, peeled and thinly sliced
- ½ cup sliced water chestnuts
- Hot cooked rice

1. Cut chicken into bite-size pieces and place in a resealable plastic bag. For marinade, mix water, soy sauce, and broth. Pour marinade over chicken in bag and seal. Marinate in the refrigerator for 30 minutes. Remove chicken; reserve the marinade. Stir cornstarch into marinade; set aside.

2. Heat oil over medium-high heat in a wok. Add green onion, mushrooms, and garlic; cook and stir 1 to 2 minutes or until tender. Remove vegetables from wok. Add chicken to wok; cook and stir 2 to 3 minutes or until no longer pink. Push chicken from center of wok. Stir marinade mixture; add to center of wok. Cook and stir until thickened and bubbly.

3. Return cooked vegetables to wok. Add water chestnuts. Cook and stir until combined. Serve with hot cooked rice. Makes 4 servings.

Per serving, with rice: 352 cal., 9 g fat (1 g sat. fat), 66 mg chol., 555 mg sodium, 34 g carbo., 3 g fiber, 32 g pro.

Challenge: We love Asian food. How can I make our favorites at home?

Cluck-Cluck BBQ Sandwiches

This recipe also tastes great with leftover cooked beef or pork.

Prep: 15 minutes **Cook:** 10 minutes

- **2 cups leftover cooked chicken breast cut into strips**
- **1 medium carrot, shredded**
- **½ cup bottled barbecue sauce**
- **4 hamburger buns, split and toasted, or one 16-ounce loaf French bread, split and toasted**
- **½ cup shredded Monterey Jack cheese (2 ounces) (optional)**
- **Pickle slices (optional)**

1. In a medium saucepan, heat the chicken, carrot, and barbecue sauce over medium heat until bubbly.

2. Spoon chicken mixture onto bottom halves of buns. If desired, top with cheese. Place on a baking sheet. Broil 3 to 4 inches from heat for 1 to 2 minutes or until cheese melts. If desired, top with pickle slices. Cover with bun tops. Makes 4 servings.

Per serving: 269 cal., 6 g fat (2 g sat. fat), 53 mg chol., 520 mg sodium, 27 g carbo., 2 g fiber, 25 g pro.

Challenge: How can I make leftover chicken taste delicious?

Extra Saucy Chicken Sandwiches

The number of people sitting down to dinner can change on a daily basis. Here's a dish that can serve just two, but also easily doubles to serve four or more.

Start to Finish: 30 minutes

- **1** **small onion, halved crosswise and thinly sliced**
- **1** **pound skinless, boneless chicken breast halves, cut into bite-size strips**
- **1** **tablespoon cooking oil**
- **½** **14- to 16-ounce jar cheddar cheese pasta sauce (about ¾ cup)**
- **1** **tablespoon Worcestershire sauce**
- **6** **slices marbled rye bread, toasted**
- **1** **small tomato, sliced**
- **6** **slices bacon, crisp-cooked and drained (optional)**

1. In a large skillet, cook onion and chicken in hot oil over medium-high heat for 4 to 5 minutes or until chicken is no longer pink. Add pasta sauce and Worcestershire sauce. Heat through.

2. To serve, spoon chicken and sauce mixture over half of the bread slices. Top with tomato and, if desired, bacon. Top with remaining bread slices. Makes 2 to 3 servings.

Note: This recipe easily doubles to serve 4 to 6 people. Multiply all the ingredients by two and prepare as directed.

Per serving: 491 cal., 18 g fat (5 g sat. fat), 114 mg chol., 1,084 mg sodium, 38 g carbo., 4 g fiber, 43 g pro.

Challenge: What can I make for two that will also easily double?

Chicken Tacos

Tweak your favorite tacos just a bit by substituting chicken for the more common beef. For grown-up tastes, top with extras like black olives, salsa, and hot sauce.

Start to Finish: 30 minutes

- **Nonstick cooking spray**
- 1 **cup chopped onion (1 large)**
- 1 **clove garlic, minced**
- 2 **cups chopped cooked chicken**
- 1 **8-ounce can tomato sauce**
- 1 **4-ounce can diced green chile peppers, drained**
- 12 **taco shells**
- 2 **cups shredded lettuce**
- ½ **cup chopped seeded tomato (1 medium)**
- ½ **cup finely shredded cheddar cheese and/or Monterey Jack cheese (2 ounces)**

1. Spray an unheated large skillet with cooking spray. Heat skillet over medium heat. Add the onion and garlic; cook until onion is tender. Stir in the chicken, tomato sauce, and chile peppers. Heat through.

2. Divide chicken mixture among taco shells. Top with lettuce, tomato, and cheese. Makes 6 servings.

Per serving: 286 cal., 13 g fat (4 g sat. fat), 51 mg chol., 473 mg sodium, 25 g carbo., 4 g fiber, 19 g pro.

Challenge: I need a new twist on kid-friendly tacos!

Chili-Lime Chicken Salad

This south-of-the-border salad has plenty of spunk with the chili powder-spiked chicken, but also an abundance of nutrition with lettuce, tomatoes, and avocadoes.

Prep: 25 minutes **Roast:** 25 minutes
Stand: 15 minutes

- 1 pound chicken tenders
- 2 teaspoons chili powder
- Salt and ground black pepper
- 1 tablespoon olive oil
- 1/4 cup olive oil or salad oil
- 3 tablespoons lime juice
- 2 tablespoons snipped fresh cilantro
- 1 tablespoon white wine vinegar
- 1/4 teaspoon salt
- Dash ground black pepper
- 6 cups torn romaine lettuce
- 8 cherry tomatoes, halved or quartered
- 1/2 of a medium avocado, pitted, peeled, and coarsely chopped

1. In a bowl, toss chicken tenders with chili powder and salt and pepper to taste. In a large skillet, heat 1 tablespoon oil over medium-high heat. Add chicken; reduce heat to medium. Cook 8 to 12 minutes or until chicken is no longer pink; turn once.

2. Meanwhile, for dressing, in a screw-top jar, combine 1/4 cup oil and the lime juice, cilantro, vinegar, 1/4 teaspoon salt, and dash pepper. Cover; shake well. Arrange lettuce on 4 salad plates. Top with chicken, tomato, and avocado. Drizzle with dressing. Makes 4 servings.

Per serving: 284 cal., 20 g fat (3 g sat. fat), 55 mg chol., 278 mg sodium, 8 g carbo., 4 g fiber, 20 g pro.

Challenge: I need a nutritious meal that isn't boring or blah.

Chicken & Grape Pasta Salad

Chill this flavorful salad for up to 24 hours so every family member gets the chance to eat a homemade dinner.

Prep: 40 minutes **Chill:** 4 hours

- **1 2- to 2½-pound deli-roasted chicken or 3 cups chopped cooked chicken**
- **1½ cups dried radiatore, mostaccioli, and/or medium shell pasta**
- **3 cups assorted fresh grapes, halved and seeded if desired**
- **1½ cups halved small strawberries**
- **1 cup chopped peeled jicama or one 8-ounce can sliced water chestnuts, drained**
- **⅔ cup bottled cucumber ranch salad dressing**
- **⅛ teaspoon cayenne pepper**
- **1 to 2 tablespoons milk (optional)**
- **Leaf lettuce**
- **Purchased sugared sliced almonds (optional)**

1. Remove skin and bones from chicken and discard. Tear chicken into bite-size pieces. Cook pasta according to package directions. Drain pasta. Rinse with cold water. Drain again.

2. In a large salad bowl, place chicken, pasta, grapes, strawberries, and jicama; toss to combine.

3. For dressing, in a small bowl, stir together dressing and cayenne pepper. Pour dressing over chicken mixture. Toss lightly to coat. Cover and chill for 4 to 24 hours.

4. Before serving, if necessary, stir in enough milk to moisten. Serve salad in lettuce-lined bowls and, if desired, sprinkle with almonds. Makes 6 servings.

Per serving: 455 cal., 20 g fat (3 g sat. fat), 67 mg chol., 269 mg sodium, 43 g carbo., 3 g fiber, 27 g pro.

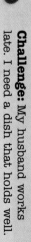

Challenge: My husband works late. I need a dish that holds well.

Mediterranean Mostaccioli

Ground beef goes to the next level with this pull-out-the-stops pasta sauce. Say goodbye to burgers!

Start to Finish: 25 minutes

- 4 ounces dried mostaccioli or gemelli pasta
- 2 cups sliced zucchini
- 8 ounces lean ground beef
- ½ of a medium eggplant, peeled and cubed (about 2½ cups)
- 1 14½-ounce can diced tomatoes with basil, oregano, and garlic, undrained
- 2 tablespoons tomato paste
- ½ cup shredded carrot
- ¼ cup snipped fresh basil
- 2 tablespoons raisins (optional)
- ¼ teaspoon ground cinnamon
- 1 tablespoon balsamic vinegar (optional)
- ½ cup shredded mozzarella cheese (2 ounces)

1. Cook pasta according to package directions, adding zucchini during the last 2 minutes of cooking. Drain; cover with foil to keep warm.

2. Meanwhile, for sauce, in a large skillet, cook beef and eggplant over medium heat until meat is brown; drain off fat. Stir in undrained tomato, tomato paste, carrot, basil, raisins (if desired), and cinnamon. Bring to boiling; reduce heat. Simmer, uncovered, about 2 minutes or to desired consistency, stirring occasionally. Remove from heat. If desired, stir in vinegar.

3. Transfer pasta mixture to a serving dish. Spoon sauce over pasta mixture. Sprinkle with cheese. Makes 4 to 6 servings.

Per serving: 334 cal., 11 g fat (5 g sat. fat), 47 mg chol., 672 mg sodium, 38 g carbo., 4 g fiber, 21 g pro.

Challenge: What else can I do with ground beef besides burgers?

Taco Pizza

This quick-fix dinner is perfect for munching on while watching movies or playing games with the family.

Prep: 15 minutes **Bake:** 20 minutes

- **8 ounces lean ground beef**
- **1 medium green sweet pepper, chopped (3/4 cup)**
- **1 11½-ounce package refrigerated corn bread twists**
- **½ cup purchased salsa**
- **3 cups shredded taco cheese (12 ounces)**
- **Crushed tortilla chips (optional)**
- **Sour cream (optional)**
- **Chopped tomato (optional)**
- **Chopped green onion (optional)**

1. Preheat oven to 400°F. In a skillet, cook beef and sweet pepper over medium heat until meat is browned; drain. Set aside.

2. Unroll corn bread dough (do not separate into strips). Press dough into the bottom and up the edges of a greased 12-inch pizza pan. Spread salsa on top of dough. Sprinkle with meat mixture and cheese. Bake about 20 minutes or until bottom of crust is golden when lifted slightly with a spatula. If desired, top with crushed tortilla chips, sour cream, tomato, and green onion. Cut into slices. Makes 6 slices.

Per slice: 451 cal., 30 g fat (15 g sat. fat), 73 mg chol., 901 mg sodium, 26 g carbo., 1 g fiber, 22 g pro.

Challenge: I need a fun meal for family movie time on Friday night!

Challenge: What is a delicious meal that serves a large family?

Saucy Meatball Sandwiches

Cooking for big families can be difficult, but not with this easy mega-batch supper.

Start to Finish: 25 minutes

- **2 eggs**
- **1½ cups soft whole wheat bread crumbs**
- **½ cup finely chopped onion**
- **½ teaspoon salt**
- **½ teaspoon dried Italian seasoning, crushed**
- **2 pounds lean ground beef**
- **2 26- to 28-ounce jars red pasta sauce**
- **12 hoagie or bratwurst buns**
- **½ cup grated Parmesan cheese**

1. Preheat oven to 350°F. In a large bowl, combine eggs, bread crumbs, onion, salt, and Italian seasoning. Add ground beef; mix well. Shape into 48 meatballs. Arrange meatballs in a large roasting pan or 15×10×1-inch baking pan. Bake for 15 to 20 minutes or until done (160°F). Drain well.

2. In a 4-quart Dutch oven, combine the pasta sauce and meatballs. Heat through. Split buns or hollow out tops of unsplit buns. Spoon hot meatball mixture into buns. Spoon any remaining sauce over the meatballs. Sprinkle cheese over the meatballs. Top with bun halves, if buns are split. Let stand 1 to 2 minutes before serving. Makes 12 servings.

Per serving: 599 cal., 18 g total fat (6 g sat. fat), 86 mg chol., 1,351 mg sodium, 83 g carbo., 6 g fiber, 29 g pro.

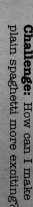

Challenge: How can I make plain spaghetti more exciting?

Contrary to popular belief, **size isn't important**. Fresh spears are tender, regardless of thickness.

Spaghetti with Shrimp, Asparagus & Tomatoes

Jazz up everyone's favorite pasta by tossing in some fresh ingredients—shrimp, asparagus, tomatoes, and basil.

Start to Finish: 30 minutes

- **4 ounces dried spaghetti**
- **12 ounces fresh or frozen peeled and deveined shrimp**
- **16 thin spears fresh asparagus**
- **1 teaspoon olive oil**
- **4 cloves garlic, minced**
- **2 cups chopped seeded plum tomato (6 medium)**
- **¼ cup chicken broth**
- **¼ teaspoon salt**
- **¼ teaspoon ground black pepper**
- **1 tablespoon butter**
- **¼ cup shredded fresh basil**

1. Cook pasta according to package directions; drain and return to pan to keep warm.

2. Meanwhile, thaw shrimp, if frozen. Set aside. Snap off and discard woody bases from asparagus. If desired, scrape off scales. Remove tips; set aside. Bias-slice asparagus stalks into 1- to 1½-inch pieces; set aside.

3. In a skillet, heat oil over medium heat. Add garlic; cook and stir for 15 seconds. Add tomato; cook and stir for 2 minutes. Add asparagus stalks, broth, salt, and pepper. Cook, uncovered, for 3 minutes. Add asparagus tips and shrimp; cook, uncovered, for 2 to 3 minutes or until shrimp are opaque. Add butter; stir until melted.

4. Add asparagus mixture and basil to pasta in pan; toss to combine. Serve warm. Makes 4 servings.

Per serving: 274 cal., 6 g fat (2 g sat. fat), 137 mg chol., 362 mg sodium, 31 g carbo., 4 g fiber, 24 g pro.

Veggie Lasagna

Oozing with reduced-fat cheese and packed with fresh vegetables, this dish gives you the best of both worlds—gooey lasagna and healthful eating.

Prep: 30 minutes **Bake:** 50 minutes
Stand: 10 minutes

- **4 cups broccoli florets, chopped carrots, chopped zucchini, and/or chopped yellow summer squash**
- **1 tablespoon olive oil**
- **1 cup light ricotta cheese or low-fat cottage cheese**
- **3 tablespoons grated Parmesan cheese**
- **¼ teaspoon ground black pepper**
- **2 cups purchased pasta sauce**
- **4 dried no-boil lasagna noodles**
- **1 cup shredded part-skim mozzarella cheese (4 ounces)**
- **½ cup cherry tomato, quartered**

1. Preheat oven to 375°F. In a large nonstick skillet, cook and stir vegetables in hot oil over medium-high heat about 10 minutes or until crisp-tender. Remove from heat and set aside. In a small bowl, stir together ricotta cheese, Parmesan cheese, and pepper.

2. To assemble, spoon about ½ cup of the pasta sauce into the bottom of a 2-quart square baking dish. Top with two of the lasagna noodles. Spread half of the ricotta cheese mixture evenly over the noodles. Top with half of the vegetable mixture, half of the remaining sauce, and half of the mozzarella cheese. Repeat layers.

3. Cover with foil. Bake for 45 minutes or until heated through and noodles are tender. Uncover; sprinkle with tomato. Bake, uncovered, 5 minutes more. Let stand for 10 minutes before serving. Makes 6 servings.

Test Kitchen Tip: If desired, add ½ cup chopped, cooked chicken on top of each vegetable mixture layer.

Per serving: 236 cal., 9 g fat (4 g sat. fat), 24 mg chol., 493 mg sodium, 25 g carbo., 4 g fiber, 13 g pro.

Challenge: We love lasagna. How can I make it more nutritious?

Vegetarian Gumbo

Bold flavors and hearty protein-packed black beans can satisfy a meat-eater's need for substance while still keeping a vegetarian's dietary restrictions in check.

Prep: 10 minutes **Cook:** 6 hours (low) or 3 hours (high)

- 2 **15-ounce cans black beans, rinsed and drained**
- 1 **28-ounce can diced tomatoes, undrained**
- 1 **16-ounce package frozen loose-pack pepper stir-fry vegetables (yellow, green, and red sweet peppers and onions)**
- 2 **cups frozen cut okra**
- 2 **to 3 teaspoons Cajun seasoning**
- **Hot cooked white or brown rice (optional)**
- **Chopped green onion (optional)**

1. In a $3\frac{1}{2}$- to $4\frac{1}{2}$-quart slow cooker, combine drained black beans, undrained tomato, frozen stir-fry vegetables, okra, and Cajun seasoning.

2. Cover and cook on low-heat setting for 6 to 8 hours or on high-heat setting for 3 to 4 hours. If desired, serve over hot cooked rice and garnish with green onion. Makes 6 servings.

Per serving: 153 cal., 0 g fat (0 g sat. fat), 0 mg chol., 639 mg sodium, 31 g carbo., 10 g fiber, 12 g pro.

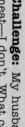

Challenge: My husband loves meat—I don't. What can I serve?

Sweet Potato Soup

A major source of vitamins A and C, sweet potatoes are an excellent ingredient to use in place of regular potatoes. Also try them as a side dish in this smooth, maple syrup-sparked soup.

Prep: 20 minutes **Cook:** 20 minutes

- ½ **cup chopped onion (1 medium)**
- ½ **cup chopped celery (1 stalk)**
- 1 **clove garlic, minced**
- 1 **tablespoon butter**
- 1 **sweet potato, peeled and cubed (about 2 cups)**
- 2 **cups reduced-sodium chicken broth**
- ½ **teaspoon ground nutmeg**
- 1½ **cups half-and-half or light cream**
- 1 **tablespoon maple syrup**
- **Dairy sour cream (optional)**
- **Ground nutmeg (optional)**

1. In a Dutch oven, cook onion, celery, and garlic in hot butter over medium heat until onion is tender but not brown. Add sweet potato, broth, and nutmeg; bring to boiling. Reduce heat; simmer, covered, 20 minutes or until potato is tender. Remove from heat; cool slightly.

2. Transfer mixture to a blender or food processor. Cover and blend or process until smooth. Return all soup to the Dutch oven. Stir in half-and-half and maple syrup; heat through. If desired, top each serving with sour cream and additional nutmeg. Makes 4 servings.

Per serving: 233 cal., 13 g fat (8 g sat. fat), 41 mg chol., 392 mg sodium, 24 g carbo., 3 g fiber, 6 g pro.

Challenge: Sweet potatoes are so healthful. How can I serve them?

Rice Pilaf with Oranges & Walnuts

For quick side dishes, rice mixes are always a good option. This sensational recipe incorporates unique ingredients to add life to meat, poultry, and seafood dishes.

Prep: 20 minutes **Cook:** 25 minutes

- 1½ **cups sliced button mushrooms (4 ounces)**
- 1 **cup sliced celery (2 stalks)**
- 1 **cup finely chopped onion (2 medium)**
- 1 **tablespoon cooking oil**
- 1 **14-ounce can chicken broth**
- ⅔ **cup water**
- 1 **6-ounce package long grain and wild rice mix**
- 2 **medium oranges, peeled and sectioned, or one 11-ounce can mandarin orange sections, drained**
- ½ **cup chopped toasted walnuts**

1. In a large saucepan, cook mushrooms, celery, and onion in hot oil over medium heat about 5 minutes or until tender. Add broth and water; bring to boiling. Stir in wild rice mix and seasoning packet; reduce heat. Cover and simmer for 25 to 30 minutes or until rice is tender. Remove from heat. Gently stir in orange and walnuts. Makes 6 servings.

Per serving: 214 cal., 10 g fat (1 g sat. fat), 1 mg chol., 673 mg sodium, 29 g carbo., 3 g fiber, 6 g pro.

Challenge: Help! I need ideas for creative side dishes!

Basil & Tomato Pasta Salad

When the summer crop of vegetables and herbs starts ripening, here's a tasty dish to try. It makes use of green beans, tomatoes, and basil from the garden (or market).

Prep: 25 minutes **Chill:** 4 hours

- **8 ounces dried pasta (such as rotini, cavatelli, or penne)**
- **6 ounces fresh green beans, trimmed and cut into 1-inch pieces, or 1 cup frozen cut green beans**
- **3 medium tomatoes, cut into thin wedges (about 1 pound)**
- **1 cup desired-flavor bottled vinaigrette salad dressing**
- **¾ cup finely shredded Parmesan cheese (3 ounces)**
- **½ cup sliced pitted kalamata olives or ripe olives**
- **½ cup finely shredded fresh basil**
- **Shaved Parmesan cheese (optional)**

1. Cook pasta according to package directions, adding green beans the last 5 minutes of cooking; drain. Rinse with cold water; drain again.

2. In a very large bowl, toss together the pasta mixture, tomato, salad dressing, shredded cheese, olives, and basil. Cover and chill for 4 to 24 hours. Toss gently before serving. If desired, top with shaved Parmesan. Makes 12 to 16 side-dish servings.

Per serving: 170 cal., 8 g fat (2 g sat. fat), 4 mg chol., 384 mg sodium, 19 g carbo., 2 g fiber, 5 g pro.

Challenge: What can I do with the produce from my garden?

Garden Pasta

This pasta toss is the perfect light meal for hot summer nights on the deck. During late summer, make use of garden-fresh veggies from the farmer's market.

Start to Finish: 25 minutes

- 4 **ounces dried spaghetti, linguine, fettuccine, or angel hair pasta or one 9-ounce package refrigerated pasta**
- 1 **medium zucchini or yellow summer squash, halved lengthwise and sliced**
- 2 **teaspoons olive oil**
- 1 **tomato, cut into thin wedges**
- 3 **to 4 tablespoons purchased basil pesto**

1. Prepare pasta according to package directions; drain.

2. In a large skillet, cook the zucchini in oil over medium heat until crisp-tender. Place pasta in serving bowl. Add tomato, pesto, and cooked zucchini. Toss gently to mix. Makes 2 servings.

Per serving: 389 cal., 15 g fat (3 g sat. fat), 7 mg chol., 226 mg sodium, 51 g carbo., 4 g fiber, 12 g pro.

Challenge: I need a light dish that's perfect for summer days.

Sugar Snap, Tomato & Feta Salad

Sauteed vegetables have outstanding flavor, without a lot of added fat or calories. Mix with mint and crumbled feta for added dimension.

Start to Finish: 15 minutes

- ½ **pound sugar snap peas or snow peas, strings removed (about 2 cups)**
- 1 **tablespoon extra virgin olive oil**
- 1 **cup grape tomatoes, halved**
- ¼ **cup fresh mint leaves, coarsely chopped**
- **Salt and ground black pepper**
- ½ **cup coarsely crumbled feta cheese**

1. In a large skillet, cook peas in hot oil over medium heat for 2 to 4 minutes over medium-high heat until crisp-tender. Stir in tomato, mint, and salt and pepper to taste. Heat through. Add cheese and toss to combine. Makes 4 to 6 servings.

Per serving: 111 cal., 8 g fat (3 g sat. fat), 17 mg chol., 359 mg sodium, 7 g carbo., 2 g fiber, 5 g pro.

Challenge: Steamed vegetables are dull. What else can I do?

Did you know?

- Tomatoes will ripen faster if they are stored in a brown paper bag, out of the sunlight, and at room temperature.
- Tomatoes are considered fruit, not vegetables, because the seeds are part of the edible plant.

a. Common Tomato
Has a sweet taste that is considered the classic tomato flavor; tastes great plain, mixed with salads or pasta, or cooked.

b. Pear Tomato
Extra juicy, small, similar in texture to cherry tomato but tastes milder (leaning more toward sweet than rich); ideal when eaten plain; also called yellow teardrop.

c. Plum Tomato
Less acidic than common tomato; sweeter flavor works well in pasta sauces and when dried; often used for the popular sun-dried variety at supermarkets; also called roma.

d. Grape Tomato
So called because of its small size and because it grows in a cluster like grapes; popular with kids because it's easy to snack on and very sweet.

e. Cherry Tomato
Favored in salad bars; sweet yet rich, and so tender you can cut it with a fork.

Challenge: I need a quick recipe for preparing asparagus.

Chilled Asparagus Salad

Fresh springtime asparagus has plenty of flavor on its own. But toss it with a few extra ingredients and it magically creates a filling side dish or light lunch.

Start to Finish: 25 minutes

- ½ **cup mayonnaise or salad dressing**
- ¼ **cup plain yogurt**
- ½ **teaspoon finely shredded orange peel**
- ⅓ **cup orange juice**
- ⅛ **teaspoon lemon-pepper seasoning**
- 1 **pound fresh asparagus spears**
- 6 **cups torn butterhead (Boston or Bibb) lettuce**
- 1 **small red onion, cut into thin wedges (½ cup)**
- 1 **11-ounce can mandarin orange sections, drained**

1. For dressing, stir together mayonnaise, yogurt, orange peel, orange juice, and lemon-pepper seasoning; set aside.

2. Snap off and discard woody bases from asparagus. In a saucepan, cook asparagus in a small amount of lightly salted boiling water for 3 to 5 minutes or until crisp-tender; drain. Plunge asparagus into ice water to chill; drain. Toss with lettuce, onion, orange sections, and dressing. Makes 4 to 6 servings.

Per serving: 277 cal., 23 g fat (4 g sat. fat), 11 mg chol., 180 mg sodium, 16 g carbo., 3 g fiber, 4 g pro.

Challenge: What is a good vegetable to toss on the grill?

Grilled Asparagus with Lemon

Long asparagus are ideal for grilling because they lie across the grill grate without falling in. Partially cooking the asparagus keeps it from burning before it's tender.

Prep: 15 minutes **Marinate:** 30 minutes **Grill:** 3 minutes

- **1 to 1½ pounds fresh asparagus spears**
- **2 tablespoons olive oil**
- **2 tablespoons lemon juice**
- **½ teaspoon salt**
- **¼ teaspoon ground black pepper**
- **Lemon wedges**

1. Snap off and discard woody bases from asparagus. If desired, scrape off scales. In a large skillet, cook the asparagus in a small amount of boiling water for 3 minutes. Drain well. Meanwhile, for marinade, in a 2-quart rectangular baking dish, stir together olive oil, lemon juice, salt, and pepper. Add drained asparagus, turning to coat. Cover and marinate at room temperature for 30 minutes. Drain asparagus, discarding marinade. Place asparagus on a grill tray or in a grill basket.

2. For a charcoal grill, grill asparagus on the rack of an uncovered grill directly over medium heat for 3 to 5 minutes or until asparagus is tender and beginning to brown, turning once halfway through grilling. (For a gas grill, preheat grill. Reduce heat to medium. Place asparagus on grill rack over heat. Cover and grill as above.)

3. To serve, arrange asparagus on a serving platter. Serve with lemon wedges. Makes 4 to 6 side-dish servings.

Per serving: 87 cal., 7 g fat (1 g sat. fat), 0 mg chol., 294 mg sodium, 7 g carbo., 3 g fiber, 3 g pro.

Home Run Garlic Rolls

Since garlic complements many savory dishes, this homemade version of garlic bread can be eaten with almost any meal.

Prep: 20 minutes **Rise:** 1½ hours
Bake: 15 minutes

1 **16-ounce loaf frozen white or whole wheat bread dough, thawed**
1 **tablespoon butter, melted**
2 **cloves garlic, minced**
2 **tablespoons grated Parmesan cheese**

1. Lightly grease a 13×9×2-inch baking pan; set aside. Shape dough into 24 balls; place in prepared pan. Cover; let rise in a warm place until nearly double (1½ to 2 hours).

2. Preheat oven to 350°F. In a small bowl, stir together melted butter and garlic. Brush butter mixture over rolls. Sprinkle with Parmesan. Bake for 15 to 20 minutes or until golden. Remove rolls from pans and cool slightly on a wire rack. Serve warm. Makes 24 rolls (12 servings).

Per serving: 55 cal., 1 g fat (0 g sat. fat), 2 mg chol., 99 mg sodium, 9 g carbo., 0 g fiber, 1 g pro.

Challenge: I need a bread I can serve with just about anything.

how to keep garlic fresh

Garlic should be stored loosely covered, away from light and heat. Freezing destroys its texture; storing it in oil at room temperature can make it poisonous. When buying fresh garlic, make sure it's free of sprouts—a sign of age.

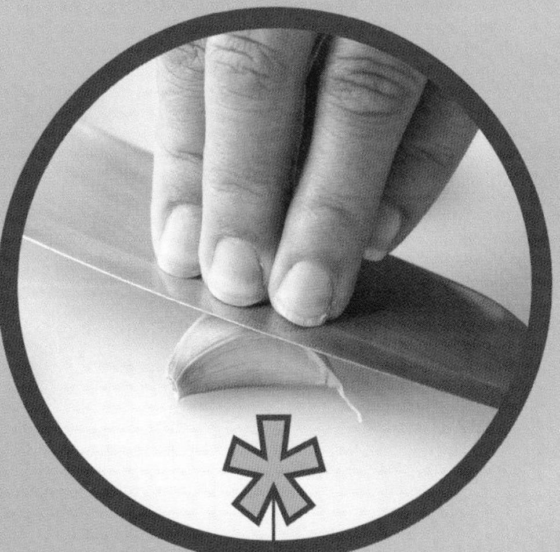

easy tip

That annoying little cling-on clove skin isn't easy to remove. Next time, push or pound the broad side of a knife against a clove—the skin comes right off!

Garlic Lovers Unite

Related to onions, shallots, and leeks, garlic grew in central Asia more than 6,000 years ago. Today it's a favorite around the world.

* **Roast it.** Roasting garlic mellows its intense raw flavor. That mellowness mixes well into homemade soups and tastes delicious when stirred in with beans and greens. Or stir it into butter or olive oil and relish with bread. Another option is to stir it into mayonnaise for a zesty sandwich spread.
* **Chop it.** A little chopped garlic goes a long way. Add it to stir-fries and sauteed vegetables or rub it on meat, seafood, or poultry before cooking. For a quick supper, try tossing a touch of it with chopped tomatoes, basil, hot cooked pasta, and/or cooked shrimp.

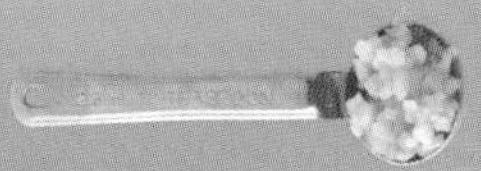

1 teaspoon minced

=

1 clove

Bet you didn't know: **Chicago** gets its name from the Native American word for a variety of **wild garlic called "chicagaoua."**

Parmesan Twists

These twists can be made savory or sweet—depending on the topping. The main recipe, Parmesan Twists, works as a side dish while the Cinnamon-Sugar Twists variation can be relished as an after-dinner sweet.

Prep: 10 minutes **Bake:** 10 minutes

1 11-ounce package (12) refrigerated breadsticks
2 tablespoons butter or margarine, melted
2 to 3 tablespoons grated Parmesan cheese
Pizza sauce or cheese dip, warmed

1. Preheat oven to 375°F. Grease a large baking sheet; set aside. Separate breadsticks. Brush each with melted butter; sprinkle with Parmesan. Twist each breadstick several times. Arrange on prepared baking sheet.

2. Bake for 10 to 13 minutes or until golden. Cool on a wire rack. Serve with pizza sauce or cheese dip for dipping. Makes 12 twists.

Cinnamon-Sugar Twists: Prepare as above except omit Parmesan and pizza sauce or cheese dip. In a small bowl, combine 2 tablespoons sugar and $\frac{1}{4}$ teaspoon ground cinnamon. Sprinkle breadsticks with sugar mixture after brushing with butter. Twist and bake as above. Serve with applesauce or fruit preserves for dipping.

Per twist (both variations): 95 cal., 3 g fat (1 g sat. fat), 5 mg chol., 199 mg sodium, 15 g carbo., 0 g fiber, 2 g pro.

Challenge: Is there anything I can serve as a side and dessert?

Corn Bread Mini Muffins

Use a corn muffin mix to make short work of homemade corn bread. A luscious honey butter spread makes it a bit more special.

Prep: 15 minutes **Bake:** 10 minutes
Cool: 5 minutes

- **Nonstick cooking spray**
- **¼ cup butter or margarine, softened**
- **1 tablespoon honey**
- **Dash cayenne pepper or several dashes bottled hot pepper sauce**
- **⅓ cup buttermilk**
- **1 egg, slightly beaten**
- **1 8.5-ounce package corn muffin mix**
- **½ cup frozen whole kernel corn, thawed**
- **½ cup shredded cheddar cheese (2 ounces)***

1. Preheat oven to 400°F. Lightly coat twenty-four 1¾-inch muffin cups with cooking spray; set aside.

2. For butter spread, in a small bowl, stir together butter, honey, and cayenne pepper; set aside.

3. In a medium bowl, stir together buttermilk and egg. Add muffin mix; stir just until moistened. Stir in corn and cheese. Spoon batter into prepared muffin cups, filling two-thirds full.

4. Bake for 10 to 12 minutes or until golden and a wooden toothpick inserted in centers comes out clean. Cool in muffin cups on a wire rack for 5 minutes. Remove from muffin cups; serve warm with butter spread. Makes 24 muffins.

*** Note:** Looking to save a few bucks? Instead of expensive packaged cheese, buy a block of cheese and shred it yourself.

Per muffin: 77 cal., 4 g fat (2 g sat. fat), 17 mg chol., 105 mg sodium, 9 g carbo., 0 g fiber, 2 g pro.

Challenge: Is there an easy way to make homemade corn bread?

make now, serve later

Make-ahead meals—whether stored for 24 hours in the fridge or 3 months in the freezer—are a guaranteed lifesaver on busy weeknights. A little forethought is required, but the reward is an easy homemade meal—just heat and eat!

Parmesan Chicken & Broccoli

Prep: 30 minutes **Bake:** 40 minutes
Freeze: up to 3 months

- **1 cup converted rice**
- **½ cup sliced green onion (4)**
- **12 ounces skinless, boneless chicken breast halves, cut into strips**
- **¾ teaspoon dried Italian seasoning, crushed**
- **1 clove garlic, minced**
- **1 tablespoon cooking oil**
- **1 16-ounce jar reduced-fat Alfredo pasta sauce**
- **3 cups frozen cut broccoli**
- **⅓ cup grated Parmesan cheese**
- **¼ cup diced cooked ham**
- **1 2-ounce jar diced pimiento, drained**
- **Ground black pepper**

1. Cook rice according to package directions; remove from heat and stir in the green onion. Divide the rice mixture among four 12- to 16-ounce au gratin dishes or casseroles; set aside.

2. In a large skillet, cook the chicken strips, Italian seasoning, and garlic in hot oil over medium heat for 4 to 6 minutes or until chicken is no longer pink. Remove from heat. Stir in Alfredo sauce, broccoli, Parmesan, ham, and pimiento. Season to taste with pepper. Spoon chicken mixture over rice in dishes. Cover with freezer wrap, label, and freeze up to 3 months.*

3. To serve, thaw frozen dishes overnight in the refrigerator. Preheat oven to 350°F. Remove freezer wrap; cover each dish with foil. Bake for 20 minutes. Uncover and bake about 20 minutes more or until heated through. Makes 4 servings.

***Note:** To serve immediately, after preparing casseroles, cover and bake in a 350°F oven for 15 minutes. Uncover and bake about 15 minutes more or until heated through.

Per serving: 660 cal., 25 g fat (12 g sat. fat), 109 mg chol., 1,277 mg sodium, 71 g carbo., 5 g fiber, 39 g pro.

Baked Penne with Meat Sauce

Prep: 30 minutes **Bake:** 75 minutes
Freeze: up to 1 month

- **8 ounces dried penne pasta**
- **1 14.5-ounce can diced tomatoes, undrained**
- **½ of a 6-ounce can (⅓ cup) Italian-style tomato paste**
- **⅓ cup dry red wine or tomato juice**
- **⅓ cup water**
- **½ teaspoon sugar**
- **½ teaspoon dried oregano, crushed, or 2 teaspoons snipped fresh oregano**
- **¼ teaspoon salt**
- **¼ teaspoon ground black pepper**
- **1 pound lean ground beef**
- **½ cup chopped onion (1 medium)**
- **¼ cup sliced pitted ripe olives**
- **1 cup shredded reduced-fat mozzarella cheese (4 ounces)**

1. Cook pasta according to package directions; drain well.

2. In a bowl, stir together undrained tomatoes, tomato paste, wine, water, sugar, dried oregano (if using), salt, and pepper.

3. In a large skillet, brown ground beef and onion over medium heat. Drain off fat. Stir in tomato mixture. Bring to boiling; reduce heat. Cover and simmer for 10 minutes. Stir in pasta, fresh oregano (if using), and olives.

4. Divide the mixture among six 10- to 12-ounce casseroles. (Or use one 3-quart rectangular baking dish.)* Cover with freezer wrap, label, and freeze up to 1 month.

5. To serve, preheat oven to 350°F. Remove freezer wrap; cover each casserole with foil. Bake about 70 minutes or until heated through. Sprinkle with mozzarella cheese. Bake, uncovered, about 5 minutes more or until cheese melts. Makes 6 servings.

***Note:** To serve in a 3-quart baking dish, after freezing, remove freezer wrap. Cover dish with foil. Bake about 1½ hours or until heated through; stir carefully once. Sprinkle with mozzarella cheese. Bake, uncovered, 5 minutes more or until cheese melts.

Per serving: 342 cal., 10 g fat (4 g sat. fat), 51 mg chol., 465 mg sodium, 37 g carbo., 2 g fiber, 22 g pro.

Bean & Beef Enchilada Casserole

Prep: 25 minutes **Bake:** 40 minutes
Chill: up to 24 hours

- **½ pound lean ground beef**
- **½ cup chopped onion (1 medium)**
- **1 teaspoon chili powder**
- **½ teaspoon ground cumin**
- **1 15-ounce can pinto beans, rinsed and drained**
- **1 4-ounce can diced green chile peppers, undrained**
- **1 8-ounce carton dairy sour cream or light sour cream**
- **2 tablespoons all-purpose flour**
- **¼ teaspoon garlic powder**
- **8 6-inch corn tortillas**
- **1 10-ounce can enchilada sauce or one 10.5-ounce can tomato puree**
- **1 cup shredded cheddar cheese (4 ounces)**
- **Chopped tomato (optional)**
- **Sliced green onion (optional)**

1. In a large skillet, cook the ground beef, onion, chili powder, and cumin over medium heat until onion is tender and meat is no longer pink. Drain off fat. Stir in drained pinto beans and undrained chile peppers; set aside.

2. In a small bowl, stir together sour cream, flour, and garlic powder; set aside.

3. Place half of the tortillas in the bottom of a lightly greased 2-quart rectangular baking dish; cut to fit if necessary. Top with half of the meat mixture, half of the sour cream mixture, half of the enchilada sauce, and ½ cup cheese. Repeat layers, except reserve remaining ½ cup cheese. Cover dish with plastic wrap; chill in refrigerator up to 24 hours.

4. To serve, preheat oven to 350°F. Remove plastic wrap; cover dish with foil. Bake 35 to 40 minutes or until bubbly. Sprinkle with reserved ½ cup cheese. Bake, uncovered, about 5 minutes more or until cheese melts. If desired, top with chopped tomato and sliced green onion. Makes 6 servings.

Per serving: 429 cal., 24 g fat (12 g sat. fat), 64 mg chol., 632 mg sodium, 36 g carbo., 6 g fiber, 15 g pro.

Chili-Cheese Hoagies

For the bold diners at your table, serve these crowd-pleasing hoagies with pickled jalapeño pepper slices.

Prep: 35 minutes **Bake:** 35 minutes
Chill: up to 24 hours

- 1 **pound lean ground beef**
- 1 **cup chopped onion (1 large)**
- 1 **cup chopped green and/or red sweet pepper (2 small)**
- 2 **cloves garlic, minced**
- 1 **14.5-ounce can diced tomatoes, undrained**
- ½ **teaspoon ground cumin**
- ¼ **teaspoon ground black pepper**
- 8 **hoagie buns or French-style rolls**
- 8 **thin slices Monterey Jack cheese or Monterey Jack cheese with jalapeño peppers (8 ounces)**
- 8 **thin slices cheddar cheese (8 ounces)**
- **Pickled jalapeño pepper slices (optional)**

1. In a large skillet, cook ground beef, onion, sweet pepper, and garlic over medium heat until meat is brown. Drain off fat. Add undrained tomato, cumin, and black pepper. Bring to boiling; reduce heat. Simmer, uncovered, about 15 minutes or until thickened, stirring occasionally. Cool the meat mixture for 30 minutes or chill until ready to assemble the sandwiches.

2. Split rolls lengthwise. Hollow out roll bottoms, leaving a ¼-inch-thick shell. Place a slice of Monterey Jack cheese, cut to fit, on bottom half of hoagie. Spoon meat mixture on top of cheese. Top meat mixture with a slice of cheddar cheese. If desired, sprinkle with pickled jalapeño pepper slices. Add hoagie top. Repeat with remaining hoagies. Wrap each sandwich in parchment paper, then in foil. Chill up to 24 hours.

3. Preheat oven to 375°F. Place wrapped hoagies on a baking sheet. Bake for 35 to 40 minutes or until cheese is melted and filling is hot. Makes 8 sandwiches.

Per serving: 738 cal., 31 g fat (15 g sat. fat), 91 mg chol., 1,274 mg sodium, 79 g carbo., 5 g fiber, 36 g pro.

Pizza Supreme

Homemade frozen pizza beats purchased frozen pizza any day. Mix and match toppings as you like.

Prep: 30 minutes **Bake:** 25 minutes

Freeze: up to 1 month

- **1 15-ounce can pizza sauce**
- **2 12-inch (10 ounces each) thin Italian bread shells* (such as Boboli) or purchased baked pizza crust**
- **1 pound bulk Italian sausage, ground beef, or ground pork, cooked and drained; or 1½ cups diced cooked ham or Canadian-style bacon (6 ounces)**
- **1 cup sliced fresh mushrooms or sliced green sweet peppers**
- **½ cup sliced green onions (4) or sliced pitted ripe olives**
- **3 cups shredded mozzarella cheese (12 ounces)**

1. Spread pizza sauce evenly on crusts. Top pizzas with meat, mushroom, green onion, and cheese.

2. Cover pizzas with plastic wrap and freeze until firm. Wrap frozen pizzas in moistureproof and vaporproof wrap. Wrap in heavy foil or place in a large resealable freezer bag; seal. Label and freeze for up to 1 month.

3. To serve, preheat oven to 375°F. Unwrap one pizza and place on baking sheet. Bake about 25 minutes or until cheese is bubbly. Makes 3 to 4 servings per pizza.

Tip: For a crisper crust, bake pizza directly on oven rack.

***Note:** If you prefer to use a thicker pizza crust, increase baking time to about 35 minutes.

Per serving: 685 cal., 37 g fat (14 g sat. fat), 100 mg chol., 1,586 mg sodium, 18 g carbo., 2 g fiber, 36 g pro.

Pork & Noodles

Prep: 30 minutes **Chill:** up to 24 hours

- 8 **ounces dried Chinese egg noodles**
- 1½ **pounds fresh asparagus spears, trimmed and cut into 2-inch-long pieces**
- 4 **medium carrots, cut into thin ribbons or bite-size strips (2 cups)**
- 1 **pound cooked lean pork, cut into thin strips**
- 1 **recipe Soy-Sesame Vinaigrette**
- **Sesame seeds (optional)**
- **Sliced green onion (optional)**

1. Cook noodles according to package directions; drain. Rinse with cold water until cool; drain.

2. If using fresh asparagus, cook in a covered saucepan in a small amount of lightly salted boiling water for 4 to 6 minutes or until crisp-tender. Drain asparagus well.

3. In a large bowl, combine noodles, asparagus, carrot, and pork. Cover and chill in the refrigerator for 2 to 24 hours.

4. To serve, prepare Soy-Sesame Vinaigrette and gently toss with mixture. If desired, sprinkle with sesame seeds and green onion. Makes 8 (1½-cup) servings.

Soy-Sesame Vinaigrette: In a screw-top jar, combine ½ cup reduced-sodium soy sauce, ¼ cup rice vinegar or vinegar, ¼ cup honey, 2 tablespoons salad oil, and 2 teaspoons toasted sesame oil. Cover and shake well to mix. Chill for 2 to 24 hours.

Per serving: 338 cal., 12 g fat (3 g sat. fat), 71 mg chol., 654 mg sodium, 35 g carbo., 3 g fiber, 23 g pro.

Baked Rotini with Ham

This creamy, colorful dish is a real kid-pleaser.

Prep: 25 minutes **Bake:** 25 minutes
Stand: 10 minutes **Chill:** up to 24 hours

- **8 ounces dried tricolor rotini (3 cups)**
- **1 16- to 17-ounce jar Alfredo pasta sauce**
- **½ cup milk**
- **½ cup shredded mozzarella cheese (2 ounces)**
- **2 ounces cooked ham, chopped (½ cup)**
- **1 teaspoon dried Italian seasoning, crushed**
- **⅛ teaspoon ground black pepper**
- **¼ cup grated Parmesan cheese**

1. Cook rotini according to package directions; drain and return to pan. Stir in Alfredo sauce, milk, mozzarella, ham, Italian seasoning, and pepper.

2. Transfer rotini mixture to four 7- to 8-ounce au gratin dishes or ramekins or a 1½-quart au gratin dish. Sprinkle with Parmesan cheese. Cover and chill for up to 24 hours.

3. To serve, preheat oven to 350°F. Cover with foil and bake for 25 to 30 minutes for the individual dishes or about 45 minutes for the casserole dish or until mixture is heated through. Let stand for 10 minutes. Stir before serving. Makes 4 servings.

Per serving: 503 cal., 28 g fat (13 g sat. fat), 121 mg chol., 1,084 mg sodium, 51 g carbo., 2 g fiber, 20 g pro.

Vegetable Shepherd's Pie

Prep: 25 minutes **Cook:** 30 minutes
Bake: 1 hour **Chill:** overnight

- **1 14-ounce can vegetable broth or chicken broth**
- **¾ cup water**
- **1 cup dry lentils, rinsed and drained**
- **3 cloves garlic, minced**
- **1½ pounds parsnips or 9 carrots, peeled and cut into ½-inch-thick slices (about 3½ cups)**
- **6 purple boiling onions (8 ounces), quartered, or 1 medium red onion, cut into wedges**
- **1 14.5-ounce can diced tomatoes with Italian herbs, undrained**
- **2 tablespoons tomato paste**
- **4 medium potatoes, peeled and cut up**
- **3 tablespoons butter or margarine**
- **1 tablespoon snipped fresh thyme or ½ teaspoon dried thyme, crushed**
- **½ teaspoon salt**
- **¼ to ⅓ cup milk**
- **1½ cups shredded Colby and Monterey Jack or cheddar cheese (6 ounces)**

1. In a large saucepan, stir together broth, water, lentils, and garlic. Bring to boiling; reduce heat. Cover and simmer for 20 minutes. Add parsnip and onion. Return to boiling; reduce heat. Cover and simmer for 10 to 15 minutes or until vegetables and lentils are just tender. Remove from heat. Stir in tomatoes and the tomato paste.

2. In a 2-quart saucepan, cook potato in lightly salted boiling water for 20 to 25 minutes or until tender; drain. Mash potato. Add butter, thyme, and salt. Gradually beat in milk until potato is light and fluffy. Stir in 1 cup of the cheese until melted.

3. Spread lentil mixture into a 2- to 2½-quart au gratin dish. Spoon potato mixture over lentil mixture. Cover dish with plastic wrap; chill in refrigerator overnight.

4. To serve, preheat oven to 350°F. Remove plastic wrap; cover dish with foil. Bake for 50 minutes. Uncover and bake for 10 to 15 minutes more or until heated through. Sprinkle with remaining ½ cup cheese. Makes 6 servings.

Per serving: 449 cal., 16 g fat (10 g sat. fat), 42 mg chol., 1,122 mg sodium, 58 g carbo., 17 g fiber, 20 g pro.

chill and store

Reheating chilled or frozen dishes is a great way to pull a meal together fast. Here are three simple tips:

* Store fragile items, such as cakes and cookies, on top of sturdy items, such as casseroles and meats.
* Thaw all foods other than baked goods in the refrigerator; baked goods can thaw at room temperature.
* Heat foods to a safe serving temperature before serving. Bring soups, sauces, and gravies to a full boil before serving. Heat all other leftovers to 165°F.

Quick freezer tip

Avoid UFOs—unidentified frozen objects—by labeling packages with the recipe name, number of servings, and date placed in the freezer.

More on storage

Below are some guidelines for chilling and freezing certain meals, but remember that not every dish will freeze well. Follow specific instructions outlined in individual recipes.

FOOD	STORE	REFRIGERATE 40°F up to:	FREEZE 0°F up to:
Casseroles	Line baking dish with heavy-duty foil. Place casserole contents in lined dish. Spray foil with nonstick spray. Wrap tightly and freeze. When frozen, lift foil-covered food out and place in freezer. To thaw, refrigerate overnight.	2–3 days	4 months
Chicken (cooked)	Package in resealable freezer bags.	2–3 days	4 months
Lasagna	See Casseroles above. Protect top of lasagna with plastic wrap or waxed paper before wrapping in foil.	2–3 days	4 months
Beef, lamb or pork (cooked)	Package in resealable freezer bags.	4 days	3 months
Soups, stews	Divide into convenient portions. Transfer to plastic freezer containers. Thaw in refrigerator for 24 hours before reheating.	4 days	3 months
Veggie, potato, or rice dishes	See Casseroles above.	3–4 days	3 months

Homemade sauces

Thick and meaty, creamy and rich—no matter what the style of sauce, it's guaranteed to add spunk to dinner.

Spicy Tomato Sauce

For even more kick on your pasta, choose a spicy Italian sausage for this sauce.

Prep: 15 minutes **Cook:** 15 minutes

- ½ **pound uncooked bulk sweet or hot Italian sausage**
- ½ **pound lean ground beef**
- ½ **cup chopped onion (1 medium)**
- 1 **teaspoon minced garlic (2 cloves)**
- 2 **14.5-ounce cans diced tomatoes with garlic and onion, undrained**
- 2 **teaspoons dried basil, crushed**
- ¼ **teaspoon crushed red pepper (optional)**
- **Hot cooked pasta**

1. In a large skillet, cook sausage, ground beef, onion, and garlic over medium heat until sausage is brown, stirring to break up meat. Drain off fat. Stir in undrained tomatoes, basil, and, if desired, crushed red pepper. Bring to boiling; reduce heat. Simmer, uncovered, for 15 to 18 minutes or until desired consistency.

2. Serve immediately or divide sauce between two airtight containers. Cover and refrigerate for up to 3 days or freeze for up to 3 months. Thaw overnight in the refrigerator before using. To serve, place desired amount of sauce in a saucepan; heat through. Serve over or toss with hot cooked pasta. Makes 4 cups.

Per ¼ cup: 83 cal., 5 g fat (2 g sat. fat), 19 mg chol., 332 mg sodium, 4 g carbo., 5 g pro.

Roasted Red Pepper Sauce

Prep: 15 minutes **Cook:** 5 minutes

- 2 12-ounce jars roasted red sweet peppers, drained
- 1 large onion, chopped
- 2 teaspoons minced garlic (4 cloves)
- 1 tablespoon olive oil
- 1 tablespoon sugar
- 1 tablespoon balsamic vinegar
- 1 teaspoon dried thyme, crushed
- ½ teaspoon dried oregano, crushed
- ¼ teaspoon salt
- ⅛ teaspoon ground black pepper
- Hot cooked pasta
- Finely shredded Parmesan cheese (optional)

1. Place drained sweet peppers in a food processor. Cover and process until smooth; set aside.

2. In a medium saucepan, cook onion and garlic in hot oil over medium-high heat until tender. Add pureed peppers, sugar, vinegar, thyme, oregano, salt, and black pepper. Cook and stir until heated through.

3. Serve immediately or divide mixture among ½-cup airtight containers. Cover and refrigerate for up to 1 week or freeze for up to 3 months. Thaw overnight in the refrigerator before using. To serve, place desired amount of sauce in a saucepan; heat through. Serve over or toss with hot cooked pasta. If desired, sprinkle with Parmesan cheese. Makes 2½ cups.

Per ½ cup: 75 cal., 3 g fat (0 g sat. fat), 0 mg chol., 120 mg sodium, 12 g carbo., 2 g fiber, 1 g pro.

Homemade Pesto

When it's time to reheat and eat, stir 2 tablespoons pesto with 1 cup hot cooked pasta.

Start to Finish: 15 minutes

- **3 cups firmly packed fresh basil leaves (3 ounces)**
- **⅔ cup walnuts**
- **⅔ cup grated Parmesan or Romano cheese**
- **½ cup olive oil**
- **4 cloves garlic, peeled and quartered**
- **½ teaspoon salt**
- **¼ teaspoon ground black pepper**

1. In a food processor or blender, combine basil, nuts, cheese, olive oil, garlic, salt, and pepper. Cover and process or blend until nearly smooth, stopping and scraping sides as necessary.

2. Place pesto in a storage container. Cover the surface with plastic wrap, then cover the container. Store in the refrigerator for 1 to 2 days. Or, to freeze in a standard ice cube tray, spoon 2 tablespoons pesto into each slot; cover tightly. Freeze for up to 3 months. Thaw at room temperature before using. Makes 1¼ cups.

Per 2 tablespoons: 365 cal., 19 g fat (3 g sat. fat), 5 mg chol., 200 mg sodium, 40 g carbo., 3 g fiber, 10 g pro.

Homemade Alfredo Sauce

A little cornstarch in this sauce keeps it from curdling after it thaws and helps it reheat to a nice, creamy consistency—perfect for pasta!

Start to Finish: 20 minutes

- **1¼ cups whipping cream**
- **1 cup chicken broth**
- **1 tablespoon cornstarch**
- **¼ teaspoon ground black pepper**
- **⅛ teaspoon ground nutmeg**
- **1 tablespoon olive oil**
- **2 teaspoons minced garlic (4 cloves)**
- **½ cup grated Parmesan cheese**
- **Hot cooked pasta**

1. In a medium bowl, stir together the cream, broth, cornstarch, pepper, and nutmeg; set aside. In a medium saucepan, heat oil over medium heat. Add garlic; cook and stir for 30 seconds. Add broth mixture; cook and stir until thickened and bubbly. Cook and stir for 2 minutes more. Stir in cheese.

2. Serve immediately or divide mixture among ½-cup airtight containers. Cover and refrigerate for up to 3 days or freeze for up to 3 months. Thaw overnight in the refrigerator before using. To serve, place desired amount of sauce in a saucepan; heat just to boiling. Serve over hot cooked pasta. Makes 2½ cups.

Per ¼ cup: 139 cal., 14 g fat (8 g sat. fat), 45 mg chol., 169 mg sodium, 2 g carbo., 0 g fiber, 2 g pro.

super-saucy

Reheating chilled or frozen sauces is a great way to pull a meal together fast—simply fix your favorite pasta, pour on the sauce, and you're ready to eat. Follow these tips for a quick, safe dinner:

* **Heat foods to a safe temperature**. Bring sauces just to boiling before serving.
* **Love the sauce but tired of the pasta?** No problem! Mix pasta sauces with ground beef for a saucy spin on sloppy joes or drizzle over chicken breasts and top with mozzarella for a low-carb dish.

Veggie tip

Pasta sauce is a great way to sneak in extra veggies. To pack in even more nutrition (plus add texture), stir canned diced tomatoes or fresh zucchini or squash into the sauce.

chill-and-store sauces

Pasta sauce is the ultimate make now, serve later dish. Most sauces refrigerate and freeze well, so make a few batches at once and stockpile them for later. Just make sure you seal your storage container tightly to avoid freezer burn.

SAUCE	STORE	FRIDGE	FREEZE	THAW
Alfredo	Divide sauce among ½-cup airtight containers and cover.	3 days	3 months	Overnight in the refrigerator
Marinara	Divide sauce among ½-cup airtight containers and cover.	1 week	3 months	Overnight in the refrigerator
Meat	Divide sauce between two airtight containers and cover.	3 days	3 months	Overnight in the refrigerator
Pesto	Spoon 2 tablespoons of sauce into each slot of a standard ice cube tray; cover tightly.	1 to 2 days	3 months	Room temperature
Wine sauce	Place sauce in storage container and cover.	3 days	Do not freeze	

quick, quicker, quickest

quick

30 minutes

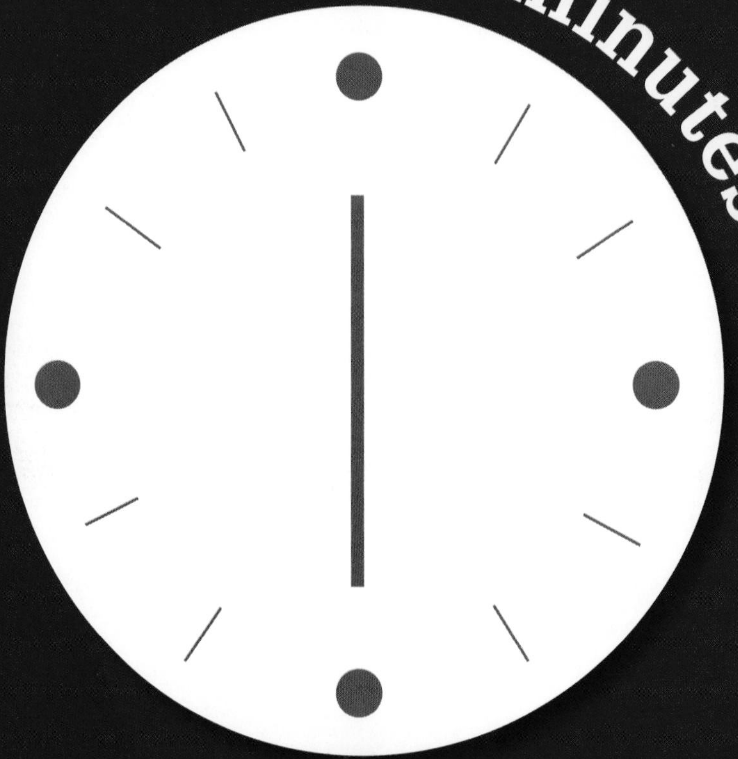

Oven-Fried Pork Chops

Coating the chops with the corn bread stuffing mix gives them a delightful, crispy crust, helping them stay juicy and moist inside.

Prep: 10 minutes **Bake:** 20 minutes

- **1 egg**
- **2 tablespoons fat-free milk**
- **1 cup packaged corn bread stuffing mix**
- **4 pork loin chops, cut ½ inch thick (1 to 1½ pounds total)**
- **1 20-ounce package frozen roasted russet potato pieces**

1. Preheat oven to 425°F. In a shallow dish, beat egg with a fork; stir in milk. Place dry stuffing mix in another shallow dish. Trim fat from chops. Dip pork chops into egg mixture. Coat both sides with stuffing mix. Arrange pork chops in a single layer on one side of 15×10×1-inch baking pan. Add potato pieces to the other side of the same pan, mounding potatoes as needed to fit.

2. Bake, uncovered, for 20 minutes or until pork is done (160°F) and potatoes are lightly browned and crisp, turning pork and stirring potatoes once. Makes 4 servings.

Per serving: 513 cal., 19 g fat (4 g sat. fat), 115 mg chol, 1,271 mg sodium, 51 g carbo., 2 g fiber, 31 g pro.

shopping list

- ❍ 8-ounce package corn bread stuffing mix
- ❍ 4 pork loin chops, cut ½ inch thick (1 to 1½ pounds total)
- ❍ 20-ounce package frozen roasted russet potato pieces

pantry items

- ❍ 1 egg
- ❍ fat-free milk

30 minutes

shopping list

- ❍ 2 medium onions
- ❍ 1 medium eggplant
- ❍ 10- or 16-ounce loose-pack frozen zucchini, carrots, cauliflower, lima beans, and Italian beans
- ❍ 14½-ounce can diced tomatoes
- ❍ seasoned salt
- ❍ 8 ounces dried penne (mostaccioli)
- ❍ 8 ounces cooked chicken

pantry items

- ❍ bottled minced garlic
- ❍ olive oil
- ❍ dried Italian seasoning
- ❍ ground black pepper

30 minutes

Chicken-Vegetable Ratatouille

Start to Finish: 30 minutes

- **1 cup chopped onion**
- **1 teaspoon bottled minced garlic**
- **1 tablespoon olive oil or cooking oil**
- **1 medium eggplant, cut into 1-inch pieces**
- **2 cups frozen zucchini, carrots, cauliflower, lima beans, and Italian beans**
- **1 14½-ounce can diced tomatoes, undrained**
- **1 teaspoon dried Italian seasoning, crushed**
- **¾ teaspoon seasoned salt**
- **¼ teaspoon ground black pepper**
- **2⅔ cups dried penne (mostaccioli), cut ziti, or wagon wheel macaroni (8 ounces)**
- **1½ cups chopped cooked chicken (about 8 ounces)**

1. In a 4-quart Dutch oven, cook onion and garlic in hot oil over medium heat for 2 minutes. Stir in eggplant, frozen vegetables, undrained tomatoes, Italian seasoning, seasoned salt, and pepper. Bring to boiling; reduce heat. Simmer, uncovered, for 10 to 12 minutes or until eggplant is tender.

2. Meanwhile, in a large saucepan, cook pasta according to package directions. Drain. Cover and keep warm.

3. Add chicken to vegetable mixture; cook about 1 minute more or until heated through. Serve chicken mixture over pasta. Makes 4 or 5 servings.

Per serving: 442 cal., 9 g fat (2 g sat. fat), 50 mg chol., 578 mg sodium, 64 g carbo., 11 g fiber, 28 g pro.

30 minutes

Stroganoff-Style Beef with Broccoli

Start to Finish: 30 minutes

- **½ cup light dairy sour cream**
- **¼ teaspoon dried dillweed**
- **1 pound boneless beef top round steak, trimmed and cut into bite-size strips**
- **1 tablespoon cooking oil**
- **1 small onion, cut into ½-inch-thick slices**
- **½ teaspoon bottled minced garlic**
- **3 cups dried wide noodles (6 ounces)**
- **3 cups broccoli florets**
- **3 tablespoons all-purpose flour**
- **1 14-ounce can beef broth**
- **3 tablespoons tomato paste**
- **1 teaspoon Worcestershire sauce**
- **Ground black pepper**

1. In a bowl, stir together sour cream and dillweed; set aside. In a skillet, cook beef in hot oil over medium-high heat until desired doneness. Remove beef; set aside. Add onion and garlic to the skillet; cook 8 to 10 minutes or until onion is tender.

2. Meanwhile, cook noodles according to package directions, adding broccoli for the last 3 minutes of cooking; drain well. Cover noodles and broccoli and keep warm.

3. Sprinkle flour over onion mixture in skillet. Stir to coat. Add broth, tomato paste, and Worcestershire sauce. Cook and stir until thickened and bubbly. Return beef to skillet; heat through. Season to taste with pepper. Remove from heat. Stir in sour cream mixture. Serve on top of noodles and broccoli. Makes 4 servings.

Per serving: 440 cal., 12 g fat (4 g sat. fat), 96 mg chol., 513 mg sodium, 45 g carbo., 4 g fiber, 37 g pro.

shopping list

- ❍ 8-ounce carton light dairy sour cream
- ❍ dried dillweed
- ❍ 1 pound boneless beef top round steak
- ❍ 1 small onion
- ❍ 6 ounces dried wide noodles
- ❍ 1 head broccoli
- ❍ 6-ounce can tomato paste

pantry items

- ❍ cooking oil
- ❍ bottled minced garlic
- ❍ all-purpose flour
- ❍ 14-ounce can beef broth
- ❍ Worcestershire sauce
- ❍ ground black pepper

30
minutes

shopping list

- ❍ two 3-ounce packages ramen noodles
- ❍ chili oil
- ❍ 12 ounces beef flank steak
- ❍ 1 piece fresh ginger
- ❍ 6- to 7-ounce bag fresh baby spinach leaves
- ❍ 6-ounce package shredded carrots
- ❍ 1 bunch fresh cilantro

pantry items

- ❍ bottled minced garlic
- ❍ 14-ounce can beef broth
- ❍ soy sauce

Asian Beef & Noodle Bowl

Start to Finish: 30 minutes

4 cups water
2 3-ounce packages ramen noodles (any flavor)
2 teaspoons chili oil or 2 teaspoons cooking oil plus ⅛ teaspoon cayenne pepper
12 ounces beef flank steak or top round steak, cut into thin, bite-size strips
1 teaspoon grated fresh ginger
1 teaspoon bottled minced garlic (2 cloves)
1 cup beef broth
2 tablespoons soy sauce
2 cups baby spinach leaves or torn fresh spinach
1 cup packaged coarsely shredded fresh carrot
¼ cup snipped fresh cilantro

1. In a large saucepan, bring the water to boiling. If desired, break up noodles; drop noodles into the boiling water. (Reserve the flavor packets for another use.) Return to boiling; boil for 2 to 3 minutes or just until noodles are tender but still firm, stirring occasionally. Drain noodles; set aside.

2. Meanwhile, in an extra-large skillet, heat oil over medium-high heat. Add beef, ginger, and garlic; cook and stir for 2 to 3 minutes or until beef is desired doneness. Carefully stir broth and soy sauce into skillet. Bring to boiling; reduce heat. Add spinach, carrot, and noodles to skillet; stir to combine. Heat through. Stir in cilantro. Makes 4 servings.

Per serving: 381 cal., 17 g fat (3 g sat. fat), 34 mg chol., 1,503 mg sodium, 30 g carbo., 2 g fiber, 26 g pro.

Beef & Veggies

Start to Finish: 30 minutes

- **12 ounces lean ground beef**
- **1 medium ($1\frac{1}{4}$ pounds) butternut squash, peeled, seeded, and cubed (about 3 cups)**
- **2 cloves garlic, minced**
- **1 teaspoon ground cumin**
- **$\frac{1}{2}$ teaspoon salt**
- **$\frac{1}{8}$ teaspoon ground cinnamon**
- **1 $14\frac{1}{2}$-ounce can diced tomatoes, undrained**
- **1 medium zucchini, halved lengthwise and sliced $\frac{1}{4}$ inch thick**
- **$\frac{1}{4}$ cup water**
- **$\frac{1}{4}$ cup chopped fresh cilantro**
- **2 to 3 cups hot cooked white or brown rice**
- **Bottled hot pepper sauce (optional)**

1. In a large skillet, cook ground beef, squash, garlic, cumin, salt, and cinnamon over medium heat until beef is no longer pink. Drain off fat.

2. Stir in undrained tomatoes; bring to boiling; reduce heat. Cover and simmer about 8 minutes or until squash is just tender. Stir in zucchini and the water. Cover and simmer about 4 minutes more or until zucchini is tender. Stir in cilantro. Serve over hot cooked rice. If desired, season to taste with bottled hot pepper sauce. Makes 4 to 6 servings.

Per serving: 313 cal., 9 g fat (3 g sat. fat), 54 mg chol., 504 mg sodium, 39 g carbo., 3 g fiber, 20 g pro.

shopping list

- ❍ 12 ounces lean ground beef
- ❍ 1 medium butternut squash
- ❍ ground cumin
- ❍ 14.5-ounce can diced tomatoes
- ❍ 1 medium zucchini
- ❍ 1 bunch fresh cilantro
- ❍ white or brown rice
- ❍ bottled hot pepper sauce (optional)

pantry items

- ❍ garlic
- ❍ salt
- ❍ ground cinnamon

30 minutes

shopping list

- ❍ 1 pound uncooked lean ground chicken
- ❍ 8-ounce package fine dry bread crumbs
- ❍ 1 loaf Texas toast
- ❍ 1 pound prepared deli coleslaw (optional)
- ❍ 12-ounce jar sliced pickles (optional)

pantry items

- ❍ egg
- ❍ salt
- ❍ ground black pepper
- ❍ olive oil
- ❍ barbecue sauce

30 minutes

Chicken Dinner Burgers

Prep: 15 minutes **Cook:** 12 minutes

1 egg, slightly beaten
½ teaspoon salt
¼ teaspoon ground black pepper
1 pound uncooked lean ground chicken or lean ground turkey
¼ cup fine dry bread crumbs
1 tablespoon olive oil
¼ cup barbecue sauce
4 slices Texas toast or other thick-sliced bread
Prepared deli coleslaw (optional)
Pickle slices (optional)

1. In a medium bowl, combine egg, salt, and pepper. Add chicken and bread crumbs; mix well. Shape the chicken mixture into four ¾-inch-thick patties.

2. In a large nonstick skillet, cook patties over medium heat in hot oil about 10 minutes or until an instant-read thermometer inserted into the thickest part of the burger registers 165°F, turning once halfway through cooking time. Brush patties on each side with barbecue sauce. Cook for 1 minute more on each side to glaze.

3. Place burgers on slices of Texas toast. If desired, top with a spoonful of coleslaw and a few pickle slices. Makes 4 servings.

Per serving: 371 cal., 17 g fat (1 g sat. fat), 103 mg chol., 912 mg sodium, 27 g carbo., 0 g fiber, 26 g pro.

30 minutes

Rice 'n' Bean Tostadas

Quick-cooking brown rice, canned chili beans, shredded cheese, and purchased tostada shells make easy work of these tostadas.

Prep: 25 minutes **Bake:** 5 minutes

- **1½ cups water**
- **1½ cups quick-cooking brown rice**
- **1 medium onion, chopped**
- **1 15-ounce can chili beans with chili gravy, undrained**
- **1 8-ounce can whole kernel corn, drained**
- **8 purchased tostada shells**
- **3 cups shredded lettuce**
- **½ cup shredded cheddar cheese (2 ounces)**
- **1 cup quartered cherry tomatoes**

1. Preheat oven to 350°F. In a saucepan, bring water to boiling. Stir in rice and onion. Return to boiling; reduce heat. Cover; simmer for 5 minutes. Remove from heat; stir. Cover; let stand for 5 minutes. Stir undrained chili beans and drained corn into rice mixture. Heat through.

2. Place tostada shells on a baking sheet. Bake for 5 minutes or until heated through.

3. To assemble, place 2 tostada shells on each dinner plate. Top tostadas with shredded lettuce and the rice-bean mixture. Sprinkle with cheddar cheese and top with tomato. Makes 4 servings.

Per serving: 438 cal., 12 g fat (4 g sat. fat), 15 mg chol., 621 mg sodium, 70 g carbo., 11 g fiber, 15 g pro.

shopping list

- ❍ 6.2-ounce package quick-cooking brown rice
- ❍ 1 medium onion
- ❍ 15-ounce can chili beans with chili gravy
- ❍ 8-ounce can whole kernel corn
- ❍ tostada shells
- ❍ 8- to 10-ounce package shredded lettuce
- ❍ 8-ounce package shredded cheddar cheese
- ❍ 1 pint cherry tomatoes

30
minutes

shopping list

- ❍ 1 package quick-cooking polenta mix
- ❍ 14-ounce can vegetable broth
- ❍ 1 large onion
- ❍ 1 head broccoli
- ❍ 7-ounce jar roasted red sweet peppers
- ❍ slivered or sliced almonds

pantry items

- ❍ cornstarch
- ❍ olive oil
- ❍ bottled minced garlic

Polenta with Broccoli

Start to Finish: 30 minutes

1 cup quick-cooking polenta mix
1 cup vegetable broth or chicken broth
1 tablespoon cornstarch
1 cup chopped onion (1 large)
4 teaspoons olive oil
3 teaspoons bottled minced garlic
3 cups coarsely chopped broccoli florets
½ of a 7-ounce jar (½ cup) roasted red sweet peppers, drained and chopped
¼ cup slivered or sliced almonds or chopped walnuts, toasted

1. Prepare polenta according to package directions. Cover and keep warm. Stir together broth and cornstarch; set aside.

2. In a large skillet, cook and stir onion in hot oil over medium heat about 4 minutes or until just tender. Add garlic; cook and stir for 30 seconds more. Add broccoli; cook and stir for 3 to 4 minutes or until crisp-tender. Stir in roasted sweet pepper.

3. Stir cornstarch mixture; add to vegetables. Cook and stir until thickened and bubbly. Cook and stir for 2 minutes more.

4. To serve, divide polenta among 4 plates. Spoon the vegetable mixture over polenta. Sprinkle with nuts. Makes 4 servings.

Per serving: 317 cal., 13 g fat (2 g sat. fat), 3 mg chol., 623 mg sodium, 45 g carbo., 6 g fiber, 10 g pro.

Grilled Steak, Mango & Pear Salad

Prep: 15 minutes **Grill:** 14 minutes

- 12 **ounces boneless beef top loin steak (1 inch thick)**
- ½ **teaspoon salt**
- ¼ **teaspoon ground black pepper**
- 1 **10-ounce package torn mixed salad greens (about 8 cups)**
- 1 **24-ounce jar refrigerated sliced mango, drained**
- 1 **medium pear, peeled, cored, and chopped**
- ¾ **cup refrigerated low-fat or fat-free blue cheese salad dressing**

1. Sprinkle both sides of steak with salt and the ¼ teaspoon ground black pepper.

2. Place steak on the rack of an uncovered grill directly over medium heat. Grill until desired doneness, turning once halfway through grilling. Allow 14 to 18 minutes for medium-rare doneness (145°F) or 18 to 22 minutes for medium doneness (160°F).

3. To serve, thinly slice steak across the grain. Arrange greens on a serving platter; top with meat, mango, and pear. Top with blue cheese salad dressing. Makes 4 servings.

Per serving: 307 cal., 5 g fat (2 g sat. fat), 50 mg chol., 900 mg sodium, 49 g carbo., 4 g fiber, 19 g pro.

shopping list

- ❍ 12 ounces boneless beef top loin steak (1 inch thick)
- ❍ 10-ounce package torn mixed salad greens
- ❍ 24-ounce jar refrigerated sliced mango
- ❍ 1 medium pear
- ❍ refrigerated blue cheese salad dressing

pantry items

- ❍ salt
- ❍ ground black pepper

30 minutes

quicker

25 minutes

25 minutes

shopping list

- ❍ 4 medium skinless, boneless chicken breast halves
- ❍ lemon-pepper seasoning
- ❍ 9-ounce package refrigerated plain linguine
- ❍ 2 medium zucchini
- ❍ apple juice
- ❍ fresh rosemary
- ❍ dry white wine
- ❍ 1 pint cherry tomatoes

pantry items

- ❍ olive oil
- ❍ bottled minced garlic
- ❍ cornstarch

Rosemary Chicken with Vegetables

Start to Finish: 25 minutes

4 medium skinless, boneless chicken breast halves
½ teaspoon lemon-pepper seasoning
2 tablespoons olive oil
4 ounces refrigerated plain linguine
1 teaspoon bottled minced garlic
2 medium zucchini and/or yellow summer squash, sliced ¼ inch thick (2½ cups)
½ cup apple juice
2 teaspoons snipped fresh rosemary or ½ teaspoon dried rosemary, crushed
2 tablespoons dry white wine or chicken broth
2 teaspoons cornstarch
1 cup halved cherry or grape tomatoes
Fresh rosemary sprigs (optional)

1. Sprinkle chicken with lemon-pepper seasoning. In a skillet, cook chicken in oil over medium heat for 8 to 10 minutes or until no longer pink; turn once. Remove chicken. Cover; keep warm. Cook pasta according to package directions.

2. Add garlic to skillet; cook for 15 seconds. Add zucchini, apple juice, and rosemary. Bring to boiling; reduce heat. Cover and simmer for 2 minutes.

3. In a bowl, stir together wine and cornstarch; add to skillet. Cook and stir until thickened and bubbly; cook for 2 minutes more. Stir in tomatoes. Serve vegetables and pasta with chicken. If desired, garnish with rosemary sprigs. Makes 4 servings.

Per serving: 326 cal., 10 g fat (2 g sat. fat), 95 mg chol., 247 mg sodium, 25 g carbo., 2 g fiber, 33 g pro.

25 minutes

shopping list

- 9-ounce package refrigerated cheese-filled ravioli
- 1 medium yellow summer squash
- 4 plum tomatoes
- 15-ounce can garbanzo beans
- fresh thyme
- 9- to 10-ounce package fresh spinach
- grated Parmesan cheese (optional)

pantry items

- bottled minced garlic
- olive oil
- ground black pepper

Ravioli with Fresh Vegetables

Start to Finish: 25 minutes

1 9-ounce package refrigerated cheese-filled ravioli or tortellini
2 teaspoons bottled minced garlic
2 teaspoons olive oil
1¼ cups thinly sliced yellow summer squash (1 medium)
4 plum tomatoes, quartered
1 15-ounce can garbanzo beans, rinsed and drained
2 teaspoons snipped fresh thyme or ½ teaspoon dried thyme, crushed
¼ teaspoon ground black pepper
4 cups shredded fresh spinach
Olive oil or cooking oil (optional)
Grated Parmesan cheese (optional)

1. Cook ravioli according to package directions; drain well.

2. Meanwhile, in a skillet, cook and stir garlic in 2 teaspoons hot oil over medium heat for 30 seconds. Add squash, tomato, garbanzo beans, thyme, and pepper. Cook and stir over medium-high heat 4 to 5 minutes or until squash is crisp-tender and mixture is heated through.

3. Add hot ravioli to vegetable mixture. Toss lightly. Arrange spinach on 4 serving plates; top with ravioli mixture. If desired, drizzle with additional olive oil and sprinkle with Parmesan cheese. Makes 4 servings.

Per serving: 304 cal., 7 g fat (2 g sat. fat), 25 mg chol., 688 mg sodium, 48 g carbo., 7 g fiber, 15 g pro.

Shrimp with Basil on Fettuccine

Start to Finish: 25 minutes

- 1 **pound frozen peeled and deveined medium shrimp (1½ pounds medium shrimp in shell)**
- 6 **ounces refrigerated spinach or plain fettuccine**
- 2 **teaspoons snipped fresh basil or tarragon or 1 teaspoon dried basil or tarragon, crushed**
- 2 **tablespoons butter or margarine**

1. Thaw shrimp, if frozen. Prepare the fettuccine according to package directions. In a large skillet, cook shrimp and basil in hot butter over medium-high heat for 2 to 3 minutes or until shrimp turn pink, stirring frequently. Serve warm over fettuccine. Makes 4 servings.

Per serving: 301 cal., 9 g fat (5 g sat. fat), 225 mg chol., 264 mg sodium, 24 g carbo., 1 g fiber, 29 g pro.

shopping list

- ❍ 1 pound frozen peeled, deveined medium shrimp
- ❍ 9-ounce package refrigerated spinach fettuccine
- ❍ fresh basil

pantry items

- ❍ butter

25 minutes

shopping list

- ❍ 10-ounce jar reduced-fat Alfredo pasta sauce
- ❍ 10-ounce package frozen peas and carrots
- ❍ 4-ounce can sliced mushrooms
- ❍ dried dillweed
- ❍ 12-ounce can tuna
- ❍ 8-ounce package biscuit mix
- ❍ 8-ounce package shredded cheddar cheese

pantry items

- ❍ lemon juice
- ❍ fat-free milk

Skillet Tuna & Biscuits

Prep: 10 minutes **Bake:** 12 minutes **Cook:** 5 minutes

- **1¼ cups Homemade Alfredo Sauce (page 57) or one 10-ounce container reduced-fat Alfredo pasta sauce**
- **1 10-ounce package frozen peas and carrots**
- **1 4-ounce can sliced mushrooms, drained**
- **1 teaspoon lemon juice**
- **¼ teaspoon dried dillweed**
- **1 12-ounce can tuna, drained and flaked**
- **1 cup packaged biscuit mix**
- **⅓ cup fat-free milk**
- **¼ cup shredded cheddar cheese (1 ounce)**

1. Preheat oven to 400°F. In a large oven-safe skillet, combine pasta sauce, peas and carrots, drained mushrooms, lemon juice, and dillweed. Cook and stir over medium heat until bubbly and heated through. Stir in drained tuna. Cover to keep warm.

2. In a medium bowl, stir together biscuit mix, milk, and half of the cheese. Drop mixture into 4 mounds on top of tuna mixture. Sprinkle with the remaining cheese.

3. Bake for 12 to 15 minutes or until biscuits are golden. Makes 4 servings.

Per serving: 434 cal., 22 g fat (10 g sat. fat), 85 mg chol., 1,032 mg sodium, 32 g carbo., 3 g fiber, 29 g pro.

25 minutes

25 minutes

shopping list

- 1 loaf country French white bread
- honey mustard
- 4-ounce block cheddar cheese
- 1 small cucumber
- fresh spinach leaves
- 1 small red onion
- 32-ounce can ready-to-serve tomato soup
- 3 medium roma tomatoes

pantry items

- olive oil
- balsamic vinegar

Smashed Veggie-Cheese Sandwiches

Prep: 20 minutes **Cook:** 3 minutes

- **8 ½-inch-thick slices country French white or wheat bread**
- **4 teaspoons olive oil or cooking oil**
- **2 tablespoons honey mustard or bottled ranch salad dressing**
- **4 ounces thinly sliced cheddar or farmer cheese**
- **½ cup thinly sliced cucumber or roma tomato**
- **½ cup fresh spinach leaves or broccoli slaw mix**
- **¼ cup thinly sliced red onion or red sweet pepper strips**
- **1 32-ounce can or bottle (4 cups) ready-to-serve tomato soup**
- **1 cup chopped roma tomato (3 medium)**
- **1 tablespoon balsamic vinegar**

1. Brush one side of bread slices lightly with oil. Brush other side of bread slices with honey mustard. Top the mustard side of four of the slices with cheese. Top cheese with cucumber, spinach, and red onion. Top with remaining bread slices, mustard sides down.

2. Preheat an indoor electric grill or a large skillet over medium heat. Place the sandwiches on the grill rack. If using a covered grill, close lid. Grill sandwiches until bread is golden and cheese is melted. (For a covered grill, allow 3 to 5 minutes. For an uncovered grill or skillet, allow 6 to 8 minutes, turning once halfway through grilling.) With a long serrated knife, cut sandwiches in half.

3. Meanwhile, in a medium saucepan stir together soup, tomato, and balsamic vinegar. Heat through. Serve soup with sandwiches. Makes 4 servings.

Per serving: 413 cal., 13 g fat (3 g sat. fat), 9 mg chol., 1,380 mg sodium, 60 g carbo., 4 g fiber, 11 g pro.

25
minutes

shopping list
- 12-ounce jar pickled peppers
- 8-ounce jar pickle relish
- 1 small onion
- poppy seeds
- 1-pound package jumbo hot dogs
- 1 package hot dog buns

pantry items
- ketchup

Saucy Dogs

Pickled peppers make these saucy hot dogs a little sassy.

Prep: 10 minutes **Grill:** 14 minutes

- **1/3 cup ketchup**
- **1/4 cup chopped pickled pepper**
- **2 tablespoons pickle relish**
- **2 tablespoons chopped onion**
- **1/4 teaspoon poppy seeds**
- **4 jumbo hot dogs (about 1 pound total)**
- **4 hot dog buns, split and toasted**

1. For sauce, in a small bowl, stir together ketchup, pickled pepper, relish, onion, and poppy seeds. Set aside.

2. For a charcoal grill, grill hot dogs on the rack of an uncovered grill directly over medium heat for 12 to 14 minutes or until heated through, turning and brushing with sauce halfway through grilling. (For a gas grill, preheat grill. Reduce heat to medium. Place hot dogs on grill rack over heat. Cover and grill as above.) Remove from grill.

3. Serve hot dogs in toasted buns; top with additional sauce. Makes 4 servings.

Per serving: 247 cal., 8 g fat (3 g sat. fat), 30 mg chol., 1,130 mg sodium, 34 g carbo., 2 g fiber, 10 g pro.

Pulled Chicken Peanut Salad

Roasted chicken from the supermarket deli and packaged washed salad greens keep the prep time for this sumptuous salad to a minimum.

Start to Finish: 25 minutes

- **2 tablespoons frozen orange juice concentrate, thawed**
- **1 tablespoon water**
- **2 teaspoons toasted sesame oil**
- **¼ teaspoon salt**
- **⅛ teaspoon coarsely ground black pepper**
- **6 cups torn mixed salad greens**
- **2 cups coarsely shredded cooked chicken**
- **1 11-ounce can mandarin orange sections, drained**
- **¼ cup cocktail peanuts**

1. For dressing, in a small bowl, stir together juice concentrate, water, sesame oil, salt, and pepper. Set aside.

2. Arrange greens on salad plates. Top with chicken, oranges, and peanuts. Drizzle with dressing. Makes 4 servings.

Per serving: 263 cal., 12 g fat (3 g sat. fat), 62 mg chol., 247 mg sodium, 15 g carbo., 2 g fiber, 24 g pro.

shopping list

- ❍ 12-ounce can frozen orange juice concentrate
- ❍ toasted sesame oil
- ❍ 10-ounce package mixed salad greens
- ❍ 1 deli chicken
- ❍ 11-ounce can mandarin orange sections
- ❍ cocktail peanuts

pantry items

- ❍ salt
- ❍ coarsely ground black pepper

25 minutes

quickest

20 minutes or less

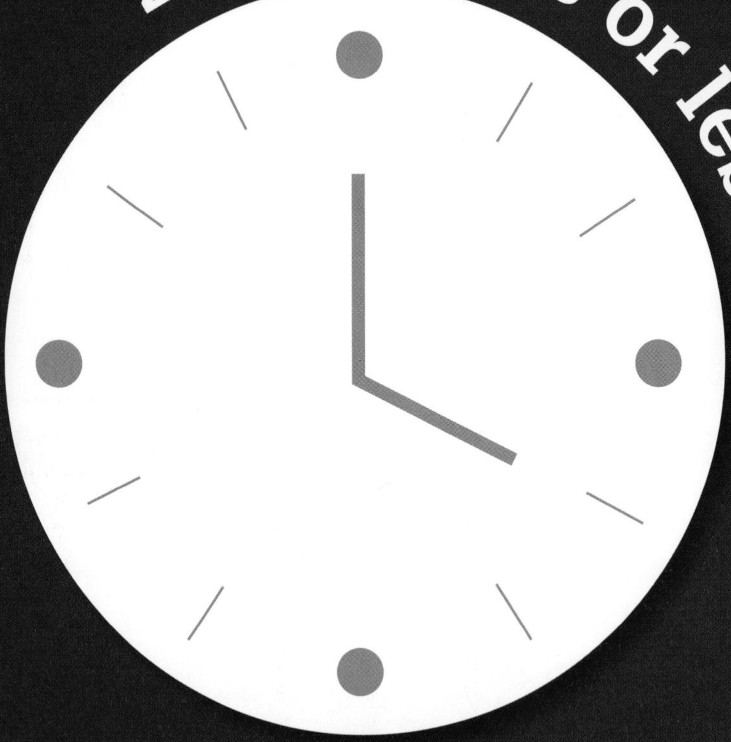

20
minutes

Apple-Pecan Pork Chops

Brown sugar and butter create a sweet sauce that marries well with pork chops and apples. Choose a tart apple for more flavor and contrast.

Start to Finish: 20 minutes

- 4 **boneless pork loin chops ($\frac{3}{4}$ to 1 inch thick)**
- **Salt and ground black pepper**
- 2 **tablespoons butter**
- 1 **medium red apple, cored and thinly sliced**
- $\frac{1}{4}$ **cup chopped pecans**
- 2 **tablespoons packed brown sugar**

1. Trim fat from pork. Sprinkle with salt and pepper. Set aside.

2. In a large skillet, melt butter over medium heat until it sizzles. Add apple; cook and stir for 2 minutes. Push apple to side of skillet. Add pork chops; cook for 4 minutes. Turn chops, moving apple aside as needed. Spoon apple over chops. Sprinkle with pecans and brown sugar.

3. Cover and cook 4 to 8 minutes more, or until an instant-read thermometer inserted in center of chops registers 160°F. Serve apple and cooking juices over chops. Makes 4 servings.

Per serving: 250 cal., 13 g fat (5 g sat. fat), 66 mg chol., 360 mg sodium, 12 g carbo., 1 g fiber, 22 g pro.

shopping list
- ❍ 4 boneless pork loin chops
- ❍ 1 medium red apple
- ❍ 1 package chopped pecans

pantry items
- ❍ salt
- ❍ ground black pepper
- ❍ butter
- ❍ brown sugar

20 minutes

shopping list

- ❍ two 15-ounce cans Great Northern beans
- ❍ 12 ounces cooked smoked ham
- ❍ 9- to 10-ounce package fresh spinach

pantry items

- ❍ olive oil
- ❍ garlic

Greens, Beans & Ham

Start to Finish: 20 minutes

2 15-ounce cans Great Northern beans
1 tablespoon olive oil
6 cloves garlic, minced
2 cups cooked smoked ham, cut into bite-size strips
3 cups chopped fresh spinach or one 10-ounce package frozen spinach, thawed and well drained

1. Drain beans, reserving liquid. In a large nonstick skillet, heat oil over medium heat. Add garlic; cook and stir for 1 minute. Add beans and ham to the skillet. Cook about 5 minutes or until heated through, stirring occasionally. Stir in spinach; cover and cook for 2 to 5 minutes more or until fresh greens are wilted or frozen spinach is heated through. If desired, thin mixture with some of the reserved liquid. Makes 4 servings.

Per serving: 353 cal., 6 g fat (1 g sat. fat), 12 mg chol., 537 mg sodium, 51 g carbo., 11 g fiber, 27 g pro.

No-Bake Tuna-Noodle Casserole

Start to Finish: 20 minutes

- **8 ounces dried cavatappi, elbow, bow-tie, or penne pasta**
- **1½ cups desired frozen vegetables (optional)**
- **¼ to ½ cup milk**
- **1 6.5-ounce container light semisoft cheese with garlic and herb**
- **1 12-ounce can solid white tuna, drained and broken into chunks**
- **Salt**
- **Ground black pepper**

1. Cook pasta in lightly salted water according to package directions. If desired, add frozen vegetables during the last 4 minutes of cooking. Drain and return to pan.

2. Add ¼ cup of the milk and the cheese to pasta in pan. Cook and stir over medium heat until cheese is melted and pasta is coated, adding additional milk as needed to create a creamy consistency. Gently fold in tuna; heat through. Season to taste with salt and pepper. Makes 4 servings.

Per serving: 419 cal., 11 g fat (6 g sat. fat), 68 mg chol., 693 mg sodium, 46 g carbo., 1 g fiber, 33 g pro.

shopping list

- ❍ 8 ounces dried cavatappi
- ❍ 9- to 10-ounce package frozen vegetables
- ❍ 6.5-ounce container semisoft cheese with garlic and herb
- ❍ 12-ounce can white tuna

pantry items

- ❍ milk
- ❍ salt
- ❍ ground black pepper

20 minutes

Add a little fun (and take away a little stress) with a food processor.

shopping list

- ❍ 1 head iceberg lettuce
- ❍ 1 medium cucumber
- ❍ 1 small sweet pepper
- ❍ 1 small red onion
- ❍ 4 ounces fresh whole mushrooms
- ❍ 2 medium carrots
- ❍ 2 ounces sharp cheddar cheese
- ❍ bottled salad dressing
- ❍ bacon (optional)

Row Salad

Start to Finish: 20 minutes

- **½ head iceberg lettuce**
- **1 medium cucumber**
- **1 small orange, red, or green sweet pepper, halved and seeded**
- **½ small red onion**
- **4 ounces fresh whole mushrooms**
- **2 medium carrots**
- **2 ounces sharp cheddar cheese**
- **1¼ cups bottled salad dressing**
- **Crumbled crisp-cooked bacon (optional)**

1. Use a food processor to slice and shred vegetables and cheese (or slice and shred ingredients by hand). If desired, cover and refrigerate salad ingredients until ready to serve.

2. To serve, arrange the vegetables and cheese in rows on a serving platter. Serve with dressing and, if desired, bacon. Makes 6 servings.

Per serving: 314 cal., 27 g fat (5 g sat. fat), 10 mg chol., 513 mg sodium, 16 g carbo., 2 g fiber, 4 g pro.

20 minutes

20
minutes

shopping list

- ❍ 1 pound boneless, skinless chicken breast tenders
- ❍ 10-ounce package torn mixed salad greens
- ❍ 1 pint fresh blueberries and/or raspberres
- ❍ fresh basil
- ❍ bottled balsamic vinaigrette salad dressing

pantry items

- ❍ cooking oil

Quick Chicken Salad with Berries

If you make this with fresh raspberries, use a bottled raspberry vinaigrette salad dressing.

Start to Finish: 20 minutes

- **1 pound boneless, skinless chicken breast tenders**
- **1 tablespoon cooking oil**
- **6 cups purchased torn mixed salad greens**
- **1½ cups fresh blueberries and/or raspberries**
- **2 tablespoons shredded fresh basil leaves**
- **½ cup bottled balsamic vinaigrette salad dressing or your favorite salad dressing**

1. In a 12-inch heavy skillet, cook chicken in hot oil over medium-high heat for 6 to 8 minutes or until no longer pink, turning once. Cool slightly. Use two forks to shred chicken.

2. In a large bowl, toss together the greens, blueberries, and basil. Drizzle vinaigrette over salad mixture; toss gently to coat. To serve, divide greens mixture among serving plates. Top with shredded chicken. Makes 6 main-dish servings.

Per serving: 194 cal., 10 g fat (1 g sat. fat), 44 mg chol., 280 mg sodium, 9 g carbo., 2 g fiber, 18 g pro.

20
minutes

shopping list

- ❍ four 10-inch flour tortillas
- ❍ toasted sesame oil
- ❍ 12 ounces lean boneless pork
- ❍ 10- or 16-ounce package loose-pack frozen stir-fry vegetables
- ❍ bottled plum sauce

Mu Shu-style Pork Roll-Ups

Start to Finish: 20 minutes

4 10-inch flour tortillas
1 teaspoon toasted sesame oil
12 ounces lean boneless pork, cut into strips
2 cups loose-pack frozen stir-fry vegetables (any combination)
¼ cup bottled plum or hoisin sauce

1. Preheat oven to 350°F. Wrap tortillas tightly in foil.Heat in oven for 10 minutes to soften. (Or wrap tortillas in microwave-safe paper towels; microwave on 100 percent power 15 to 30 seconds or until tortillas are softened.)

2. Meanwhile, in a large skillet, heat oil over medium-high heat. Add pork strips; cook and turn for 2 to 3 minutes or until done. Add stir-fry vegetables. Cook and stir for 3 to 4 minutes or until vegetables are crisp-tender.

3. Spread each tortilla with 1 tablespoon of the plum sauce; place a quarter of the meat mixture just below t he center of each tortilla. Fold the bottom edge of each tortilla up and over the filling. Fold in the sides until they meet; roll up over the filling. Makes 4 servings.

Per serving: 296 cal., 8 g fat (2 g sat. fat), 53 mg chol., 325 mg sodium, 32 g carbo., 1 g fiber, 22 g pro.

Deli-style Submarines

Use a single type of meat or pile on an assortment in this meal-size sandwich. Ranch-flavor sour cream dip adds a little extra zip.

Start to Finish: 20 minutes

- **1 16-ounce loaf French bread**
- **½ of an 8-ounce carton light dairy sour cream ranch dip**
- **1 cup shredded lettuce**
- **¾ cup shredded fresh carrot**
- **8 ounces thinly sliced cooked roast beef, ham, or turkey**
- **½ of a medium cucumber, seeded and shredded**
- **4 ounces thinly sliced mozzarella or provolone cheese**

1. Cut French bread in half horizontally. Spread ranch dip on cut sides of bread. On the bottom half of the bread, layer lettuce, carrot, roast beef, cucumber, and cheese. Replace top half of bread. Cut sandwich into 8 portions. Secure portions with decorative toothpicks. Makes 8 servings.

Make-Ahead Directions: Prepare as directed, except do not cut sandwich into pieces. Wrap sandwich in plastic wrap and chill for up to 4 hours. Cut and serve as directed.

Per serving: 250 cal., 6 g fat (3 g sat. fat), 24 mg chol., 743 mg sodium, 34 g carbo., 2 g fiber, 14 g pro.

shopping list

- ❍ 16-ounce loaf French bread
- ❍ 8-ounce carton light dairy sour cream ranch dip
- ❍ 10-ounce bag shredded lettuce
- ❍ 10-ounce bag shredded fresh carrot
- ❍ 8 ounces thinly sliced roast beef
- ❍ 1 medium cucumber
- ❍ 4 ounces thinly sliced mozzarella cheese

20 minutes

shopping list

- ❍ fresh thyme
- ❍ 1 small red onion
- ❍ 12 ounces cut-up cooked chicken
- ❍ 4 baked biscuits

pantry items

- ❍ honey

Honey Chicken Sandwiches

Start to Finish: 20 minutes

- **3 tablespoons honey**
- **2 teaspoons snipped fresh thyme or ½ teaspoon dried thyme, crushed**
- **1 small red onion, halved and thinly sliced**
- **12 ounces cut-up cooked chicken**
- **4 baked biscuits, split**

1. In a medium skillet, combine honey and thyme; stir in red onion. Cook and stir over medium-low heat just until hot (do not boil). Stir in chicken; heat through. Arrange chicken mixture on biscuit bottoms. Add tops. Makes 4 servings.

Per serving: 342 cal., 12 g fat (3 g sat. fat), 76 mg chol., 443 mg sodium, 31 g carbo., 1 g fiber, 27 g pro.

20 minutes

15
minutes

shopping list

- ❍ 1 package 8- or 9-inch plain flour tortillas
- ❍ 10-ounce jar low-fat mayonnaise
- ❍ fresh basil
- ❍ 12 ounces thinly sliced cooked chicken
- ❍ 7-ounce jar roasted red sweet peppers

pantry items

- ❍ garlic
- ❍ cayenne pepper (optional)

Basil Chicken Wraps

Start to Finish: 15 minutes

4 8- or 9-inch plain flour tortillas or tomato- or spinach-flavor flour tortillas
½ cup Basil Mayonnaise
Fresh basil leaves
12 ounces thinly sliced cooked chicken cut into thin strips
½ cup roasted red sweet pepper, cut into thin strips

1. Place the stack of flat tortillas on foil; wrap tightly. Heat in a 350°F oven until warm.
2. Prepare Basil Mayonnaise; spread onto warm tortillas. Arrange basil leaves, chicken, and sweet pepper on tortillas. Fold up bottoms; roll up. Makes 4 servings.

Basil Mayonnaise: Stir together ½ cup low-fat mayonnaise or salad dressing, 1 tablespoon snipped fresh basil, and 1 small clove garlic, minced. If desired, stir in ⅛ teaspoon cayenne pepper. Makes about ½ cup.

Per wrap: 366 cal., 15 g fat (3 g sat. fat), 44 mg chol., 1,330 mg sodium, 37 g carbo., 2 g fiber, 21 g pro.

15
minutes

shopping list

- ❍ 1 pound creamy deli coleslaw
- ❍ 1 small tomato
- ❍ curry powder
- ❍ 6-ounce can tuna
- ❍ peanuts
- ❍ 4 ciabatta rolls
- ❍ 1 head butterhead lettuce (Bibb or Boston)
- ❍ 8-ounce container dairy sour cream dip with chives (optional)

Curried Tuna Sandwiches

Start to Finish: 15 minutes

1½ cups creamy deli coleslaw
1 small tomato, seeded and chopped
1 teaspoon curry powder
1 6-ounce can tuna, drained and flaked
¼ cup chopped peanuts
4 ciabatta rolls, sliced horizontally
4 large butterhead (Bibb or Boston) lettuce leaves
Dairy sour cream dip with chives (optional)

1. In a small bowl, stir together coleslaw, tomato, and curry powder. Fold in drained tuna and chopped peanuts.

2. To serve, spoon the tuna mixture into sliced ciabatta rolls and top with lettuce leaves. If desired, top with dip. Makes 4 servings.

Tip: If you don't love curry, this sandwich fix-up works well with other combinations too. Substitute ranch seasoning for the curry powder and chopped cucumber for the chopped peanuts for a rich and creamy sandwich with a little crunch.

Per serving: 254 cal., 9 g fat (2 g sat. fat), 21 mg chol., 434 mg sodium, 28 g carbo., 3 g fiber, 17 g pro.

Twisted Tuna Salad

Start to Finish: 15 minutes

- 1 **12-ounce can chunk white tuna (water-pack), drained**
- ⅓ **cup bottled creamy Italian salad dressing**
- ⅓ **cup finely chopped fresh or canned pineapple, drained**
- ¼ **cup finely chopped red sweet pepper**
- 4 **to 8 Boston lettuce leaves**
- 2 **pita bread rounds, halved**

1. In a medium bowl, combine drained tuna, salad dressing, drained pineapple, and sweet pepper. Place the lettuce leaves in the pita halves. Fill each pita half with tuna mixture. Makes 4 servings.

Per serving: 275 cal., 11 g fat (2 g sat. fat), 36 mg chol., 819 mg sodium, 21 g carbo., 1 g fiber, 23 g pro.

shopping list

- ❍ 12-ounce can chunk white tuna (water-pack)
- ❍ bottled creamy Italian salad dressing
- ❍ 1 fresh pineapple
- ❍ 1 red sweet pepper
- ❍ 1 head Boston lettuce
- ❍ 1 package pita bread rounds

15 minutes

shopping list

- ❍ 10-ounce jar low-fat mayonnaise
- ❍ fresh basil
- ❍ 16 ounces chopped cooked chicken
- ❍ grated Parmesan cheese
- ❍ 3 green onions
- ❍ 1 celery stalk
- ❍ 1 loaf sliced wheat bread

pantry items

- ❍ lemon juice
- ❍ salt
- ❍ ground black pepper

10 minutes

Parmesan Chicken Salad Sandwiches

Start to Finish: 10 minutes

- **½ cup low-fat mayonnaise**
- **1 tablespoon lemon juice**
- **2 teaspoons snipped fresh basil**
- **2½ cups chopped cooked chicken or turkey**
- **¼ cup grated Parmesan cheese**
- **¼ cup thinly sliced green onion**
- **3 tablespoons finely chopped celery**
- **Salt**
- **Ground black pepper**
- **12 slices wheat bread, toasted**

1. For dressing, in a small bowl, stir together mayonnaise, lemon juice, and basil. Set aside.

2. For salad, in a medium bowl, combine chicken, cheese, green onion, and celery. Pour dressing over chicken mixture; toss to coat. Season to taste with salt and pepper. Serve immediately or cover and chill in the refrigerator for 1 to 4 hours. Serve on toasted wheat bread. Makes 6 main-dish servings.

Per serving: 194 cal., 12 g fat (3 g sat. fat), 61 mg chol., 366 mg sodium, 2 g carbo., 0 g fiber, 18 g pro.

10
minutes

shopping list

- ❍ frozen peas
- ❍ 8.8-ounce package cooked brown or white rice
- ❍ 1 pound chicken breast tenders
- ❍ bottled stir-fry sauce
- ❍ packaged oven-roasted sliced almonds

pantry items

- ❍ cooking oil

Fast Chicken & Rice

High heat and thin pieces of chicken make for a short cooking time. Use your favorite stir-fry sauce to tie it all together.

Start to Finish: 10 minutes

½ cup frozen peas
1 8.8-ounce package cooked brown or white rice (microwave pack)
1 pound chicken breast tenders, halved crosswise
1 tablespoon cooking oil
¼ cup bottled stir-fry sauce
Packaged oven-roasted sliced almonds

1. Stir peas into rice pouch. Heat rice pouch according to package directions.

2. Meanwhile, in a large skillet, cook and stir chicken in hot oil over medium-high heat for 2 to 3 minutes or until no longer pink. Stir rice mixture into skillet. Stir in stir-fry sauce; heat through. Sprinkle each serving with sliced almonds. Makes 4 servings.

Per serving: 311 cal., 9 g fat (1 g sat. fat), 66 mg chol., 453 mg sodium, 25 g carbo., 2 g fiber, 31 g pro.

10
minutes

shopping list

- 16-ounce package coleslaw mix
- 6 ounces sliced cooked turkey breast
- 3-ounce package ramen noodles
- bottled vinaigrette salad dressing
- 11- or 15-ounce can mandarin orange sections
- toasted sliced almonds (optional)

Quick & Crunchy Turkey Salad

Start to Finish: 10 minutes

1 16-ounce package coleslaw mix
6 ounces sliced cooked turkey breast, diced
1 3-ounce package ramen noodles
⅔ cup bottled vinaigrette salad dressing
1 11- or 15-ounce can mandarin orange sections, drained
Toasted sliced almonds (optional)

1. In a large salad bowl, combine the slaw mixture and turkey. Remove seasoning packet from noodles; reserve for another use. Crumble noodles and add to slaw mixture. Pour the dressing over the salad; toss to coat. Gently fold in orange sections. If desired, top with almonds. Makes 4 main-dish servings.

Per serving: 326 cal., 14 g fat (1 g sat. fat), 15 mg chol., 895 mg sodium, 31 g carbo., 3 g fiber, 12 g pro.

express lane recipes

Deli-roasted chicken has been your go-to plan for a quick dinner many a night, but here are some great ways to amp up the already succulent flavor.

Pulled Chicken Sandwiches

Prep: 25 minutes **Cook:** 7 minutes

- **1 2½-pound deli-roasted chicken**
- **1 medium onion, cut into ¼-inch-thick slices**
- **1 tablespoon olive oil**
- **⅓ cup cider vinegar or white wine vinegar**
- **½ cup tomato sauce**
- **3 to 4 tablespoons seeded and finely chopped fresh red and/or green hot chile pepper**
- **2 tablespoons snipped fresh thyme**
- **2 tablespoons molasses**
- **2 tablespoons water**
- **½ teaspoon salt**
- **4 sandwich buns, split**

1. Remove meat from chicken (discard skin and bones). Use two forks to shred meat (2½ to 3 cups).

2. In a large skillet, cook onion in hot oil over medium heat 5 minutes or until tender; stir to separate rings. Add vinegar; cook 1 minute more. Stir in tomato sauce, chile, thyme, molasses, 2 tablespoons water, and ½ teaspoon salt. Bring to boiling. Add chicken; stir to coat. Heat through. Serve on buns. Makes 4 sandwiches.

Per sandwich: 445 cal., 12 g fat (3 g sat. fat), 84 mg chol., 990 mg sodium, 51 g carbo., 2 g fiber, 33 g pro.

Mexican Chicken Casserole

Prep: 15 minutes **Bake:** 15 minutes

- **1 15-ounce can black beans, rinsed and drained**
- **½ cup chunky salsa**
- **½ teaspoon ground cumin**
- **1 2½-pound deli-roasted chicken**
- **¼ cup shredded Monterey Jack cheese with jalapeño peppers**
- **Dairy sour cream (optional)**

1. Preheat oven to 350°F. In a small bowl, stir together drained beans, ¼ cup of the salsa, and the cumin. Divide bean mixture among 4 au gratin dishes or casseroles. Set aside.

2. Cut chicken into quarters. Place one piece on bean mixture in each dish. Spoon remaining ¼ cup salsa evenly over chicken pieces. Sprinkle evenly with cheese. Bake for 15 to 20 minutes or until heated through. If desired, top with sour cream. Makes 4 servings.

Per serving: 468 cal., 23 g fat (7 g sat. fat), 140 mg chol., 596 mg sodium, 16 g carbo., 5 g fiber, 50 g pro.

Chicken Linguine with Pesto Sauce

Start to Finish: 20 minutes

8 ounces dried linguine
1 10-ounce package frozen vegetables
1 10-ounce container refrigerated Alfredo pasta sauce or 1 cup jarred Alfredo sauce
⅓ cup purchased basil pesto
¼ cup milk
½ of a 2½-pound deli-roasted chicken
Grated Parmesan cheese

1. In a 4-quart Dutch oven, cook pasta according to package directions; add vegetables during last 5 minutes of cooking. Drain; return to Dutch oven.
2. Meanwhile, combine Alfredo sauce, pesto, and ¼ cup milk; set aside. Remove meat from chicken (discard skin and bones). Shred meat (2½ cups).
3. Add chicken to pasta and vegetables in Dutch oven. Add sauce mixture; toss gently to coat. Heat through over medium-low heat. If desired, stir in additional milk to reach desired consistency. Sprinkle each serving with cheese. Makes 4 servings.

Per serving: 801 cal., 48 g fat (4 g sat. fat), 109 mg chol., 546 mg sodium, 54 g carbo., 3 g fiber, 37 g pro.

Chicken Quesadillas

Start to Finish: 25 minutes

1 2½-pound deli-roasted chicken
4 8- to 10-inch flour tortillas
Fresh spinach leaves
1 8-ounce can sliced mushrooms, drained
2 cups shredded Monterey Jack cheese
Salsa (optional)
Guacamole (optional)

1. Remove meat from chicken (discard skin and bones). Chop meat, reserving 2 cups. Cover and chill or freeze remaining meat for another use.
2. Spoon the 2 cups chicken evenly on bottom halves of tortillas. Top with spinach and drained mushrooms. Sprinkle cheese evenly over mushrooms. Fold tortillas in half. Heat on a griddle over medium heat until browned on both sides and cheese is melted. If desired, serve with salsa and guacamole. Makes 4 servings.

Per serving: 472 cal., 28 g fat (15 g sat. fat), 120 mg chol., 513 mg sodium, 18 g carbo., 2 g fiber, 37 g pro.

Kids love 'em for their taste, moms love 'em for their ease. These five recipes bring both attributes of breaded chicken pieces to the table in new ways.

Southwest Chicken Wraps

Start to Finish: 20 minutes

- ½ of a 28-ounce package frozen cooked, breaded chicken strips (about 24 strips)
- ½ of an 8-ounce tub light cream cheese
- 1 green onion, thinly sliced
- 1 tablespoon snipped fresh cilantro
- 6 7- to 8-inch flour tortillas
- 1 red sweet pepper, seeded and cut into bite-size strips
- ½ cup shredded reduced-fat or regular Monterey Jack cheese (2 ounces)
- Bottled salsa (optional)

1. Bake chicken strips according to directions.

2. Meanwhile, in a small bowl, stir together the cream cheese, green onion, and cilantro. Spread over tortillas. Top with pepper strips and shredded cheese. Top with hot chicken strips. Roll up tortillas; secure tortillas with toothpicks. Cut in half to serve. Serve with salsa, if desired. Makes 6 servings.

Per serving: 356 cal., 20 g fat (6 g sat. fat), 54 mg chol., 610 mg sodium, 27 g carbo., 1 g fiber, 18 g pro.

Chicken Salad with Strawberries

Any shape of frozen cooked chicken would work in this salad. Change the fruit according to what's in season, such as apples, pears, oranges, or grapes.

Start to Finish: 20 minutes

- 1 11-ounce package frozen cooked, breaded chicken nuggets or strips
- 1 10-ounce package mixed salad greens
- 2 cups sliced fresh strawberries
- ¼ cup fresh basil leaves, cut into strips
- ½ cup bottled balsamic vinaigrette salad dressing

1. Bake chicken nuggets according to package directions.

2. Meanwhile, in a very large bowl, toss together the greens, strawberries, and basil. Divide among serving plates and top with chicken. Drizzle salad dressing over the top. Makes 6 main-dish servings.

Per serving: 244 cal., 15 g fat (3 g sat. fat), 29 mg chol., 487 mg sodium, 19 g carbo., 2 g fiber, 8 g pro.

Easy Chicken Marinara

Start to Finish: 25 minutes

- **4 frozen cooked, breaded chicken breast patties**
- **2 cups purchased marinara sauce**
- **½ to 1 cup shredded mozzarella cheese (2 to 4 ounces)**
- **Hot cooked spaghetti**

1. Place chicken patties on a baking sheet. Bake according to package directions. Meanwhile, pour sauce into a saucepan and heat through over medium heat.

2. Remove baking sheet from oven; turn chicken patties over. Spoon about ¼ cup sauce over each chicken patty. Top each with cheese. Return to oven and bake for 4 to 5 minutes more or until cheese melts.

3. Serve chicken patties over spaghetti with remaining sauce. Makes 4 servings.

Per serving: 283 cal., 15 g fat (4 g sat. fat), 36 mg chol., 919 mg sodium, 24 g carbo., 3 g fiber, 14 g pro.

Chicken with Buttermilk Gravy

Lemon peel adds flavor and character to this comfort-food recipe. Another time, try it with orange peel.

Start to Finish: 15 minutes

- **6 frozen cooked, breaded chicken breast patties**
- **1 24-ounce package refrigerated mashed potatoes**
- **1 1-ounce envelope chicken gravy mix**
- **1 cup buttermilk**
- **¼ to ½ teaspoon finely shredded lemon peel**
- **¼ teaspoon dried sage, crushed**

1. Bake chicken patties according to package directions. Heat potatoes according to package directions.

2. Meanwhile, in a small saucepan, prepare chicken gravy mix according to package directions, except use the 1 cup buttermilk in place of the water called for and add lemon peel and sage. Place chicken patties on serving plates. Mound potatoes on top of patties. Spoon some of the gravy over the top. Pass remaining gravy. Makes 6 servings.

Per serving: 301 cal., 13 g fat (3 g sat. fat), 26 mg chol., 776 mg sodium, 33 g carbo., 2 g fiber, 14 g pro.

Sweet & Sour Chicken

Either breaded or grilled chicken breast strips or nuggets would work well in this recipe.

Prep: 15 minutes **Cook:** 5 minutes

- **1 11-ounce package frozen cooked, breaded chicken strips or nuggets**
- **1 tablespoon cooking oil**
- **1 medium red sweet pepper, cut into bite-size strips**
- **½ cup thinly sliced carrot (1 medium)**
- **1 cup fresh pea pods, tips and stems removed**
- **1 8-ounce can pineapple chunks, undrained (juice pack)**
- **½ cup bottled sweet-and-sour sauce**
- **2 to 3 cups hot cooked rice**

1. Bake chicken strips according to package directions.
2. Meanwhile, in a large nonstick skillet, heat oil over medium-high heat. Add sweet pepper and carrot; cook and stir for 3 minutes. Add pea pods; cook and stir about 1 minute more or until vegetables are crisp-tender.
3. Add undrained pineapple chunks and sweet-and-sour sauce to skillet; heat through. Spoon vegetable mixture over hot cooked rice and top with chicken. Makes 4 to 6 servings.

Per serving: 371 cal., 10 g fat (2 g sat. fat), 19 mg chol., 460 mg sodium, 56 g carbo., 2 g fiber, 13 g pro.

Soups, stir-fries, sandwiches, and more—
power up five creative meals with these
irresistible little bites of protein.

Meatballs Stroganoff

Start to Finish: 30 minutes

- **1 12- to 16-ounce package frozen cooked meatballs**
- **1 cup lower-sodium beef broth**
- **1 4-ounce can sliced mushrooms, drained**
- **1 8-ounce carton dairy sour cream**
- **2 tablespoons all-purpose flour**
- **½ cup milk**
- **1 tablespoon Dijon-style mustard**
- **4 cups hot cooked wide egg noodles**
- **fresh parsley (optional)**

1. In a large skillet, combine meatballs, broth, and drained mushrooms. Bring to boiling; reduce heat. Cover; simmer 15 minutes or until heated through.

2. In a bowl, stir together sour cream and flour. Whisk in milk and mustard. Stir sour cream mixture into skillet. Cook and stir until thickened and bubbly; simmer 1 minute more. Serve over hot cooked noodles. If desired, stir in snipped *fresh parsley*. Makes 6 to 8 servings.

Per serving: 424 cal., 25 g fat (12 g sat. fat), 73 mg chol., 696 mg sodium, 36 g carbo., 3 g fiber, 16 g pro.

Meatball & Red Pepper Pasta

Start to Finish: 30 minutes

- **1 cup thinly sliced carrot (2 medium)**
- **½ cup chopped onion (1 medium)**
- **2 cloves garlic, minced**
- **1 tablespoon olive oil or cooking oil**
- **2 12-ounce packages frozen cooked Italian-style meatballs (24 meatballs)**
- **1 26-ounce jar spicy red pepper pasta sauce**
- **8 ounces dried spaghetti or bow-tie pasta**
- **Finely shredded Parmesan cheese**

1. In a large skillet, cook carrot, onion, and garlic in hot oil over medium heat for 5 minutes or until tender. Stir in meatballs and pasta sauce. Bring to boiling; reduce heat. Simmer, covered, 15 minutes or until meatballs are heated through.

2. Cook pasta according to package directions until just tender; drain. Serve meatballs and sauce over hot cooked pasta. Sprinkle with Parmesan cheese. Makes 6 servings.

Per serving: 591 cal., 31 g fat (13 g sat. fat), 77 mg chol., 1,225 mg sodium, 46 g carbo., 8 g fiber, 26 g pro.

Quick Meatball Minestrone

Start to Finish: 25 minutes

- 1 **12- to 16-ounce package frozen cooked Italian-style meatballs**
- 3 **14-ounce cans lower-sodium beef broth**
- 1 **15- to 16-ounce can Great Northern or cannellini beans, rinsed and drained**
- 1 **14.5-ounce can diced tomatoes with basil, garlic, and oregano, undrained**
- 1 **10-ounce package frozen mixed vegetables**
- 1 **cup dried small pasta (such as macaroni)**
- 1 **teaspoon sugar**

1. In a 4-quart Dutch oven, stir together meatballs, broth, drained beans, undrained tomatoes, and vegetables. Bring to boiling. Stir in pasta. Return to boiling; reduce heat. Simmer, uncovered, about 10 minutes or until pasta is tender and meatballs are heated through. Stir in sugar. Makes 6 to 8 servings.

Per serving: 413 cal., 15 g fat (7 g sat. fat), 40 mg chol., 1,242 mg sodium, 47 g carbo., 8 g fiber, 24 g pro.

Sweet & Sour Meatballs

Start to Finish: 30 minutes

- 1 **20-ounce can pineapple chunks**
- ¾ **cup maple syrup or maple-flavor syrup**
- ½ **cup cider vinegar**
- 1 **12- to 16-ounce package frozen cooked meatballs**
- 2 **medium red sweet peppers**
- ¼ **cup cold water**
- 2 **tablespoons cornstarch**
- ½ **teaspoon salt**
- 2 **cups hot cooked Asian noodles or rice**

1. Drain pineapple; reserve liquid. In a large saucepan, stir together pineapple liquid, syrup, and vinegar. Add meatballs. Bring to boiling; reduce heat. Simmer, covered, for 15 minutes.

2. Remove seeds from sweet peppers and cut into ¾-inch pieces. Add to meatballs. Simmer, covered, for 5 minutes.

3. In a bowl, stir together water, cornstarch, and salt until smooth. Stir into meatball mixture. Cook and stir 1 to 2 minutes or until thickened and bubbly. Stir in pineapple chunks; heat through. Serve over hot cooked noodles. Makes 4 servings.

Per serving: 667 cal., 23 g fat (9 g sat. fat), 30 mg chol., 972 mg sodium, 107 g carbo., 5 g fiber, 14 g pro.

Meatball Hoagies

For easier eating, choose smaller ½-ounce meatballs when making these sandwiches.

Start to Finish: 30 minutes

- 1 medium onion, thinly sliced
- 1 medium red or green sweet pepper, seeded and cut into thin strips
- 1 tablespoon olive oil
- 1 16-ounce package frozen cooked Italian meatballs
- 2 cups refrigerated marinara sauce
- ¼ teaspoon crushed red pepper
- 6 slices provolone cheese (6 ounces)
- 6 hoagie buns or ciabatta rolls, split

1. In a saucepan, cook onion and sweet pepper in hot oil over medium heat for 4 to 5 minutes or until crisp-tender. Add meatballs, marinara sauce, and crushed red pepper. Bring to boiling; reduce heat. Simmer, covered, about 15 minutes or until meatballs are heated through.

2. To serve, place provolone cheese on bottom halves of rolls. Spoon meatball mixture onto each roll. If desired, broil sandwiches 4 to 5 inches from heat for 1 to 2 minutes or until cheese melts. Makes 6 sandwiches.

Per serving: 696 cal., 29 g fat (11 g sat. fat), 44 mg chol., 1,642 mg sodium, 84 g carbo., 7 g fiber, 26 g pro.

Hamburgers are great—but every night?
Keep ground beef from becoming a bummer
with these six fresh choices.

French Onion Burgers

Prep: 20 minutes **Broil:** 14 minutes

- 1 **tablespoon olive oil**
- 3 **cups sliced onion (3 large)**
- 1/4 **teaspoon salt**
- 3/4 **teaspoon coarsely ground black pepper**
- 1 1/2 **pounds lean ground beef**
- 2 **tablespoons Worcestershire sauce**
- 2 **cloves garlic, minced**
- 3/4 **cup shredded Swiss cheese or reduced-fat Swiss cheese (3 ounces)**
- 4 **3/4-inch-thick slices French bread**

1. In a skillet, heat oil over medium heat. Add onion; cook 10 minutes or until golden, stirring occasionally. Stir in salt and 1/4 teaspoon of the pepper. Cover and keep warm.

2. Meanwhile, in a large bowl, combine beef, Worcestershire sauce, the remaining 1/2 teaspoon pepper, and the garlic. Divide beef mixture into 8 equal portions. Shape each portion into a 4-inch-diameter patty. Place one-fourth of the cheese on each of four of the patties. Top with remaining patties, pressing down lightly and sealing edges to enclose cheese.

3. Place burgers on the unheated rack of a broiler pan. Broil 4 inches from the heat for 14 to 18 minutes or until done (160°F), turning once halfway through broiling.

4. Add bread slices to pan for the last 1 to 2 minutes of broiling or until toasted, turning once. Serve patties on toasted bread slices topped with onions. Makes 4 servings.

Per serving: 535 cal., 27 g fat (11 g sat. fat), 127 mg chol., 576 mg sodium, 32 g carbo., 2 g fiber, 40 g pro.

Easy Goulash

Prep: 20 minutes **Cook:** 6 hours (low) or 3 hours (high) **Stand:** 5 minutes

- 1 **pound lean ground beef**
- 1/2 **of a 24-ounce package frozen loose-pack diced hash brown potatoes with onions and peppers (about 3 1/2 cups)**
- 1 **15-ounce can tomato sauce**
- 1 **14.5-ounce can diced tomatoes with basil, garlic, and oregano, undrained**
- 1/2 **cup shredded cheddar cheese (2 ounces)**
- **Hot cooked noodles**

1. In a large skillet, cook ground beef over medium heat until brown. Drain off fat.

2. In a 3 1/2- or 4-quart slow cooker, stir together meat, frozen potatoes, tomato sauce, and undrained tomatoes.

3. Cover and cook on low-heat setting for 6 to 8 hours or on high-heat setting for 3 to 4 hours. Turn off cooker. Sprinkle cheese over meat mixture. Let stand about 5 minutes or until cheese melts. Serve with noodles. Makes 4 servings.

Per serving: 535 cal., 33 g fat (14 g sat. fat), 109 mg chol., 1,371 mg sodium, 34 g carbo., 4 g fiber, 27 g pro.

Polenta with Italian Beef Stew

Prep: 25 minutes **Cook:** 15 minutes

- 1 pound lean ground beef
- 1 14.5-ounce can diced tomatoes with basil, garlic, and oregano, undrained
- 3 medium carrots, cut into ½-inch slices
- 2 medium onions, cut into thin wedges
- 1 large red sweet pepper, cut into 1-inch pieces
- ½ cup beef broth
- 3 tablespoons tomato paste
- ¼ teaspoon salt
- ¼ teaspoon ground black pepper
- 1 teaspoon bottled minced garlic
- 1 medium zucchini, halved lengthwise and cut into ¼-inch slices
- ⅓ cup purchased basil pesto or Homemade Pesto (page 59)
- 1 16-ounce tube refrigerated cooked polenta

1. In a large skillet, cook ground beef over medium heat until brown. Drain off fat. Stir in undrained tomatoes, carrot, onion, sweet pepper, beef broth, tomato paste, salt, black pepper, and garlic. Bring to boiling; reduce heat. Cover and simmer for 10 to 15 minutes or until carrot is tender. Stir in zucchini and pesto. Cover and simmer 5 minutes more.

2. Meanwhile, prepare polenta according to package directions. Serve meat mixture with polenta. Makes 6 servings.

Per serving: 362 cal., 16 g fat (3 g sat. fat), 50 mg chol., 978 mg sodium, 34 g carbo., 5 g fiber, 20 g pro.

Chili Macaroni

Start to Finish: 30 minutes

- **12** **ounces lean ground beef or uncooked ground turkey**
- **1/2** **cup chopped onion (1 medium)**
- **1** **14.5-ounce can diced tomatoes and green chiles, undrained**
- **1 1/4** **cups tomato juice**
- **2** **teaspoons chili powder**
- **1/2** **teaspoon garlic salt**
- **1** **cup dried wagon wheel macaroni**
- **1** **cup frozen cut green beans**
- **1** **cup shredded cheddar cheese (4 ounces)**
- **Tortilla chips**

1. In a very large skillet, cook ground beef and onion over medium heat until meat is brown. Drain off fat. Stir undrained tomatoes, tomato juice, chili powder, and garlic salt into meat mixture. Bring to boiling. Stir in pasta and green beans. Return to boiling; reduce heat. Cover and simmer about 15 minutes or until pasta and beans are tender.

2. Top with shredded cheddar cheese and serve with tortilla chips. Makes 4 servings.

Per serving: 443 cal., 20 g fat (9 g sat. fat), 83 mg chol., 881 mg sodium, 37 g carbo., 5 g fiber, 29 g pro.

Upside-Down Pizza Casserole

Put the crust on top of this "pizza" by topping the ground beef mixture with biscuits.

Prep: 20 minutes **Bake:** 15 minutes

- **1 1/2** **pounds lean ground beef**
- **1** **15-ounce can Italian-style tomato sauce**
- **1 1/2** **cups shredded mozzarella cheese (6 ounces)**
- **1** **10-ounce package refrigerated biscuits (10 biscuits)**

1. Preheat oven to 400°F. In a large skillet, cook ground beef over medium heat until brown. Drain off fat. Stir in tomato sauce; heat through. Transfer beef mixture to a 2-quart rectangular baking dish or 10-inch deep-dish pie plate. Sprinkle with cheese. Flatten each biscuit with your hands; arrange the biscuits on top of cheese.

2. Bake, uncovered, about 15 minutes or until biscuits are golden. Makes 10 small or 5 large servings.

Per small serving: 321 cal., 20 g fat (8 g sat. fat), 58 mg chol., 551 mg sodium, 15 g carbo., 1 g fiber, 17 g pro.

Greek-Style Lasagna

Prep: 45 minutes **Bake:** 35 minutes
Stand: 10 minutes

- **9 dried lasagna noodles**
- **1 pound lean ground beef or lamb**
- **1 medium onion, chopped (½ cup)**
- **2 cloves garlic, minced**
- **1 8-ounce can tomato sauce**
- **¼ cup dry red wine or beef broth**
- **1 teaspoon dried oregano, crushed**
- **¼ teaspoon ground cinnamon**
- **3 tablespoons butter**
- **3 tablespoons all-purpose flour**
- **¼ teaspoon ground black pepper**
- **1¾ cups milk**
- **½ cup grated Parmesan cheese**
- **1 2¼-ounce can sliced pitted ripe olives, drained**
- **8 ounces crumbled feta cheese**
- **1 cup shredded white cheddar cheese (4 ounces)**

1. Preheat oven to 350°F. Cook noodles according to package directions; drain. Rinse with cold water; drain well and set aside.

2. In a large skillet, brown meat, onion, and garlic. Drain off fat. Stir in tomato sauce, wine, oregano, and cinnamon. Bring to boiling; reduce heat. Simmer, uncovered, 10 minutes.

3. In a saucepan, melt butter; stir in flour, pepper, and milk. Cook and stir until thickened and bubbly; cook and stir 1 minute more. Stir in Parmesan; set aside.

4. To assemble, layer noodles, meat sauce, cheese sauce, olives, and cheeses. Bake, uncovered, about 35 to 40 minutes or until heated through. Let stand 10 minutes before serving. Makes 12 servings.

Per serving: 330 cal., 20 g fat (11 g sat. fat), 67 mg chol., 516 mg sodium, 19 g carbo., 1 g fiber, 17 g pro.

food safety 101

how to handle ground beef

As the list of health concerns grows and prevention measures seem more daunting, it's comforting to know one ailment is relatively easy to stop: foodborne illness.

Simply wash your hands, wash food prep surfaces, cook food to at least 160°F, and store food smartly. That's it. No pricey prescriptions or 12-step programs.

Concerns about *E. coli* bacteria are common (perhaps rivaled only by worries about salmonella). But you don't have to give up the delicious, hearty flavor of ground beef out of fear of contamination. Follow these four easy steps to dine on hamburgers, goulash, chili, and meatballs without a care:

* Wash your hands for at least 20 seconds in warm, soapy water before and after working with any raw beef product.

* Make sure any surface—cutting board, countertop, etc.—is clean before food prep begins. Wash surfaces immediately after working with any raw beef product. If possible, use two cutting boards—one for cutting meat, the other for chopping vegetables.

* Cook ground beef to at least 160°F. Check the temperature with a clean meat thermometer. Immediately refrigerate or freeze any leftovers in a sealed container. Reheat leftover ground beef to at least 165°F.

* Don't cross-contaminate. Trays or tubes of ground beef can leak juices into the shopping cart or refrigerator. Separate raw meat from fresh produce in the cart and the fridge, and place containers in plastic bags to keep juices contained. At home, store raw meat on the bottom shelf in the refrigerator to keep juices from dripping onto other items.

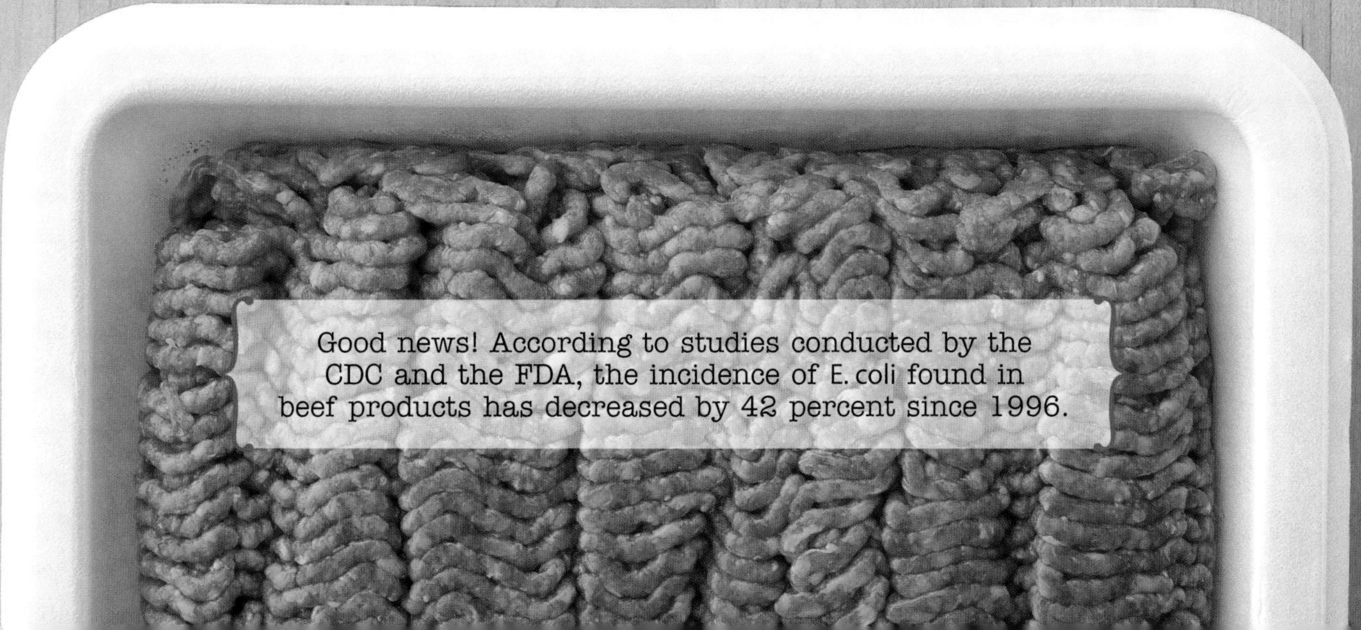

Good news! According to studies conducted by the CDC and the FDA, the incidence of E. coli found in beef products has decreased by 42 percent since 1996.

Quick-frozen shrimp is one of the fastest (and best tasting) ways to get dinner on the table. Here are five choices to make your workweek "shrimp-ilicious."

Shrimp Gumbo

Start to Finish: 40 minutes

8 ounces bulk hot Italian sausage
1 large onion, chopped
1 large green sweet pepper, chopped
2 stalks celery, thinly sliced
3 cloves garlic, chopped
2 14½-ounce cans reduced-sodium stewed tomatoes, undrained
1 14-ounce can reduced-sodium chicken broth
1 teaspoon paprika
¼ teaspoon ground black pepper
⅛ to ¼ teaspoon cayenne pepper
1 pound frozen uncooked medium shrimp, thawed, peeled, and deveined
1 cup instant white rice

1. Cook sausage, onion, sweet pepper, and celery until sausage is browned. Drain. Add garlic, undrained tomatoes, broth, paprika, black pepper, and cayenne. Bring to boiling; reduce heat. Simmer, covered, for 10 minutes.

2. Add shrimp; cook, covered, 4 minutes more, until shrimp are opaque. Remove from heat. Stir in rice. Cover; let stand 5 minutes. Serve hot. Makes 6 servings.

Per serving: 338 cal., 14 g fat (5 g sat. fat), 144 mg chol., 971 mg sodium, 28 g carbo., 4 g fiber, 24 g pro.

Mexican Shrimp Tostadas

Start to Finish: 20 minutes

4 purchased tostada shells
2 cups shredded lettuce
1 15-ounce can black beans, drained
20 frozen cooked large shrimp, thawed, peeled, and deveined
1 tablespoon lime juice
1 medium tomato, cut into 16 thin wedges
¼ cup dairy sour cream
Sliced green onion
Salsa

1. Place one tostada shell on each of 4 serving plates. Top with some lettuce and one-fourth of the beans. Arrange 5 shrimp in a circle over the drained beans; sprinkle shrimp with lime juice.

2. Arrange 4 tomato wedges on each tortilla and top with a tablespoon of the dairy sour cream and some green onion. Serve with salsa. Makes 4 servings.

Per serving: 273 cal., 6 g fat (2 g sat. fat), 227 mg chol., 670 mg sodium, 25 g carbo., 6 g fiber, 32 g pro.

Jerk-Spiced Shrimp with Wilted Spinach

Start to Finish: 25 minutes

- **12 ounces frozen uncooked medium shrimp, thawed, peeled, and deveined**
- **1½ teaspoons Jamaican jerk seasoning**
- **3 cloves garlic, minced**
- **2 tablespoons olive oil**
- **8 cups torn fresh spinach**

1. Rinse shrimp; pat dry with paper towels. In a small bowl, toss together shrimp and jerk seasoning; set aside.

2. In a large skillet, cook garlic in 1 tablespoon of hot oil for 15 to 30 seconds. Add half of the spinach. Cook and stir about 1 minute or until spinach is just wilted. Transfer to a serving platter. Repeat with remaining spinach. Cover; keep warm.

3. Carefully add remaining oil to skillet. Add shrimp. Cook and stir for 2 to 3 minutes or until shrimp are opaque. Spoon shrimp over wilted spinach. Makes 4 servings.

Per serving: 159 cal., 8 g fat (1 g sat. fat), 129 mg chol., 315 mg sodium, 2 g carbo., 6 g fiber, 19 g pro.

Shrimply Divine Pasta

Start to Finish: 20 minutes

- **1 6-ounce package rotini**
- **1½ teaspoons bottled minced garlic**
- **1 tablespoon olive oil**
- **12 ounces frozen uncooked medium shrimp, thawed, peeled, and deveined**
- **1 cup chicken broth**
- **1 tablespoon cornstarch**
- **1 teaspoon Italian herb seasoning**
- **4 cups packaged baby spinach**
- **Finely shredded Parmesan cheese**

1. Cook pasta according to package directions. Drain; keep warm. Rinse shrimp; pat dry.

2. In a skillet, cook garlic in oil over medium-high heat for 15 seconds. Add shrimp. Cook for 2 to 3 minutes or until shrimp are opaque. Remove shrimp. Add broth, cornstarch, and Italian seasoning to skillet. Cook and stir until thickened and bubbly. Add spinach. Cook until wilted. Return shrimp to skillet; stir. Toss with pasta and Parmesan cheese. Makes 4 servings.

Per serving: 333 cal., 7 g fat (1 g sat. fat), 136 mg chol., 422 mg sodium, 39 g carbo., 3 g fiber, 25 g pro.

Grilled Shrimp Kabobs

For fiery flavor, slather the kabobs with a hot and spicy variety of barbecue sauce.

Prep: 20 minutes
Grill: 6 minutes

- **1 pound frozen large shrimp in shells**
- **1 medium green and/or red sweet pepper, cut into 16 pieces**
- **¼ of a medium fresh pineapple, cut into chunks**
- **4 green onions, cut into 2- to 3-inch pieces**
- **¼ cup bottled low-carb barbecue sauce**

1. Thaw shrimp. Peel and devein shrimp, keeping tails intact. Rinse shrimp; pat dry with paper towels. Alternately thread shrimp, sweet pepper pieces, pineapple chunks, and green onions onto 8 long metal or wood skewers.

2. For a charcoal grill, grill kabobs on the greased grill rack of an uncovered grill directly over medium coals for 6 to 10 minutes or until shrimp are opaque, turning once and brushing with barbecue sauce halfway through grilling. (For a gas grill, preheat grill. Reduce heat to medium. Place kabobs on greased grill rack over heat. Cover and grill as above.) Makes 4 servings.

Per serving: 127 cal., 2 g fat (0 g sat. fat), 129 mg chol., 257 mg sodium, 9 g carbo., 1 g fiber, 18 g pro.

They're not just for snacking anymore! Introduce easy-to-prepare fish sticks to the dinner table with five kickin' meal ideas.

Fish Tacos

Start to Finish: 20 minutes

- 1 11-ounce package (18) frozen baked, breaded fish sticks
- 3 tablespoons low-fat mayonnaise or salad dressing
- 1 teaspoon lime juice
- 1½ cups packaged shredded cabbage with carrot (coleslaw mix)
- 8 corn tortillas
- Mango Salsa

1. Bake fish according to package directions. Cut each fish stick in half crosswise.
2. Meanwhile, in a bowl, stir together mayonnaise and lime juice. Add cabbage; toss to coat. Divide coleslaw mixture among tortillas. Add fish and top with mango salsa. Makes 4 servings.

Mango Salsa: In a bowl, stir together 1 cup seeded, peeled, and chopped mango; ¾ cup finely chopped red sweet pepper; ¼ cup sliced green onion; ½ teaspoon finely shredded lime peel; 1 tablespoon lime juice; ¼ teaspoon salt; and ¼ teaspoon ground black pepper. Makes 1½ cups.

Per serving: 334 cal., 12 g total fat (2 g sat. fat), 22 mg chol., 655 mg sodium, 47 g carbo., 4 g fiber, 10 g pro.

Pizza-Style Fish Sticks

Don't knock 'em before you try 'em! These wacky-sounding sticks are delicious!

Prep: 15 minutes **Bake:** 20 minutes

- 1 11-ounce package (18) frozen baked, breaded fish sticks
- 1 8-ounce can pizza sauce
- 1 cup shredded provolone or mozzarella cheese (4 ounces)
- 2 tablespoons shredded fresh basil (optional)

1. Preheat oven to 425°F. Arrange fish sticks in a 2-quart square or rectangular baking dish. Spoon sauce over sticks. Sprinkle with cheese. Bake, uncovered, about 20 minutes or until heated through. Sprinkle with basil, if desired. Makes 4 servings.

Per serving: 336 cal., 20 g fat (7 g sat. fat), 36 mg chol., 839 mg sodium, 22 g carbo., 1 g fiber, 17 g pro.

Something's Fishy Sandwiches

Prep: 10 minutes **Bake:** per package directions

- 1 11-ounce package (18) frozen baked, breaded fish sticks
- 4 thin slices tomato
- ½ teaspoon dried basil, crushed
- ⅛ teaspoon ground black pepper
- 1 cup shredded mozzarella, cheddar, Swiss, or American cheese (4 ounces)
- 2 tablespoons desired creamy salad dressing
- 4 kaiser rolls, split and toasted

1. Arrange fish sticks close together on a baking sheet. Bake according to package directions.
2. Top fish with tomato slices. Sprinkle with basil and pepper; top with cheese. Bake for 2 to 3 minutes more or until cheese is melted.
3. Spread salad dressing on bottoms of rolls. Add fish and top halves of rolls. Makes 4 servings.

Per serving: 414 cal., 14 g fat (5 g sat. fat), 35 mg chol., 875 mg sodium, 50 g carbo., 1 g fiber, 20 g pro.

Spinach & Fish Salad

Start to Finish: 25 minutes

- 1 11-ounce package (18) frozen baked, breaded fish sticks
- 4 cups baby spinach leaves
- 1 medium onion, cut into thin wedges
- 1 tablespoon olive oil or cooking oil
- 1 medium red or yellow sweet pepper, cut into thin strips
- 3 tablespoons balsamic vinegar
- 1 tablespoon honey

1. Bake fish according to package directions. Place spinach in a bowl. Top with fish; cover to keep warm.
2. Meanwhile, in a skillet, cook onion in hot oil over medium heat 5 to 6 minutes or until tender and slightly golden. Add sweet pepper; cook and stir 1 minute more. Remove from heat. Add onion mixture to spinach and fish; toss to combine. Transfer to a serving platter.
3. In a bowl, stir together the balsamic vinegar and honey. Add to skillet. Cook and stir until heated through, about 1 minute. Spoon vinegar mixture over fish and spinach. Makes 4 servings.

Per serving: 279 cal., 14 g fat (2 g sat. fat), 25 mg chol., 356 mg sodium, 29 g carbo., 3 g fiber, 10 g pro.

Sweet & Sour Fish Sticks

Start to Finish: 25 minutes

- **¾ cup bottled sweet-and-sour sauce**
- **1 11-ounce package (18) frozen baked, breaded fish sticks**
- **1 red sweet pepper, cut into strips**
- **1 tablespoon cooking oil**
- **1 cup snow pea pods, trimmed**
- **1 8.8-ounce pouch cooked brown or white rice**

1. Set aside ¼ cup of the sweet-and-sour sauce in a small microwave-safe bowl or measuring cup. Bake fish sticks according to package directions.

2. Meanwhile, in a large skillet, cook pepper strips in hot oil over medium-high heat for 3 minutes. Add pea pods and cook for 1 to 2 minutes more or until vegetables are crisp-tender. Stir in the remaining ½ cup sauce to coat; heat through. Prepare rice according to package directions.

3. Heat reserved sauce in microwave on 100-percent power (high) for 30 to 40 seconds or until heated through. Serve vegetable mixture over rice. Top with fish sticks. Drizzle with warm sauce. Makes 4 servings.

Per serving: 406 cal., 17 g fat (3 g sat. fat), 16 mg chol., 643 mg sodium, 52 g carbo., 2 g fiber, 11 g pro.

Hash brown potatoes—they're not just for breakfast anymore! Add some extra ingredients for flavor and heartiness, and this potato favorite can be transformed into four satisfying meals.

Pork & Potato Skillet

This one-pan dinner is perfect for a busy weeknight.

Start to Finish: 30 minutes

- 4 **4-ounce boneless pork loin chops**
- ¾ **teaspoon seasoned salt**
- 2 **tablespoons cooking oil**
- ⅓ **cup chopped onion (1 small)**
- 1 **medium red sweet pepper, cut into ¾-inch pieces**
- 3 **cups frozen diced hash brown potatoes**
- 2 **cups frozen peas and carrots**
- 1 **teaspoon dried thyme, crushed**

1. Sprinkle both sides of pork chops evenly with ½ teaspoon of the seasoned salt. In a very large skillet, heat 1 tablespoon of the oil over medium-high heat. Cook chops in hot oil for 3 minutes. Turn chops. Cook for 3 minutes more or until brown. Remove chops from skillet.

2. Carefully add remaining 1 tablespoon oil to skillet. Add onion and sweet pepper; cook and stir for 1 minute. Add potatoes, peas and carrots, thyme, and remaining ¼ teaspoon seasoned salt; mix well. Cook for 6 minutes, stirring frequently.

3. Place chops on top of potato mixture in skillet; cover. Reduce heat to medium. Cook for 7 to 9 minutes more or until chops are no longer pink and potatoes are brown. Makes 4 servings.

Per serving: 406 cal., 15 g fat (3 g sat. fat), 72 mg chol., 422 mg sodium, 39 g carbo., 5 g fiber, 29 g pro.

Grilled Potato & Onion Packets

Start to Finish: 30 minutes

- 1 teaspoon dried thyme, crushed
- ½ teaspoon garlic salt
- ½ teaspoon paprika
- ⅛ teaspoon ground black pepper
- Nonstick cooking spray
- 4 cups frozen diced hash brown potatoes
- 1 sweet onion, halved and thinly sliced
- 2 tablespoons olive oil
- ¼ cup dairy sour cream and chive dip (optional)

1. For seasoning mixture, stir together thyme, garlic salt, paprika, and pepper; set aside. Fold a 48×18-inch piece of heavy foil in half to make a double thickness of foil that measures 24×18 inches. Lightly coat the foil with cooking spray.

2. Place potatoes and onion in center of foil. Drizzle potatoes and onions with oil. Sprinkle with seasoning mixture.

3. Bring up opposite edges of foil; seal with a double fold. Fold remaining edges to enclose the vegetables, leaving space for steam.

4. For a charcoal grill, grill the foil packet on the rack of an uncovered grill directly over medium heat for 20 to 25 minutes or until the potatoes are tender. (For a gas grill, preheat grill. Reduce heat to medium. Place packet on grill rack over heat. Cover and grill as above.) If desired, serve with dip. Makes 4 to 6 servings.

Per serving: 329 cal., 20 g fat (6 g sat. fat), 0 mg chol., 161 mg sodium, 36 g carbo., 3 g fiber, 4 g pro.

Shredded Potatoes with Sausage & Apples

Start to Finish: 30 minutes

- 2 tablespoons olive oil
- 2 tablespoons butter
- 5 cups frozen shredded hash brown potatoes
- 1 tablespoon snipped fresh thyme or 1 teaspoon dried thyme, crushed
- ¼ teaspoon ground black pepper
- 6 ounces cooked smoked sausage, coarsely chopped
- 1 medium apple, such as Golden Delicious, cut into thin wedges
- Salt to taste

1. In a 10-inch cast-iron or nonstick skillet, heat the oil and 1 tablespoon of the butter over medium heat. Add potatoes in an even layer. Cook for 8 minutes, stirring occasionally, until lightly browned. Stir in half of the thyme and the pepper. With a wide metal spatula, press potatoes down firmly. Cook about 8 minutes more or until potatoes are tender.

2. Meanwhile, in a medium skillet, melt the remaining 1 tablespoon butter over medium heat. Add sausage and apple. Cook about 10 minutes or until apple is tender, stirring occasionally. Stir in remaining thyme.

3. Cut potato mixture into 4 wedges and place on serving plates; top wedges with apple mixture. Add salt to taste. Makes 4 servings.

Per serving: 365 cal., 28 g fat (10 g sat. fat), 47 mg chol., 381 mg sodium, 21 g carbo., 2 g fiber, 8 g pro.

Hash Brown Casserole

Prep: 20 minutes **Bake:** 50 minutes

- 1 10.75-ounce can reduced-fat and reduced-sodium condensed cream of chicken soup or condensed cream of chicken soup
- 1 8-ounce carton light dairy sour cream or dairy sour cream
- 4 cups frozen shredded hash brown potatoes
- 1 cup diced cooked ham (4 ounces)
- 1 cup cubed American cheese (4 ounces)
- ¼ cup chopped onion
- ⅛ teaspoon ground black pepper
- 1 cup cornflakes
- 3 tablespoons butter, melted

1. Preheat oven to 350°F. In a large bowl, stir together soup and sour cream. Stir in frozen potatoes, ham, cheese, onion, and pepper. Spread the mixture evenly into a 2-quart square baking dish. In a small bowl, combine cornflakes and butter. Sprinkle over potato mixture.

2. Bake, uncovered, for 50 to 55 minutes or until hot and bubbly. Let stand for 10 minutes before serving. Makes 6 servings.

Per serving: 351 cal., 19 g fat (11 g sat. fat), 63 mg chol., 953 mg sodium, 35 g carbo., 2 g fiber, 13 g pro.

How do you get five servings of vegetables a day? Keep it easy and delicious, and you'll have no problem getting your fill.

Crumb-Topped Vegetables

Get the kids involved in making this side dish by letting them crush the crackers in the bag.

Start to Finish: 10 minutes

- **1 12-ounce package frozen cut green beans in microwavable steaming bag (such as Birds Eye Steamfresh)**
- **1 cup cheese-flavor crackers, crushed**
- **½ teaspoon dried thyme, crushed**
- **2 tablespoons butter, melted**
- **¼ cup finely shredded Parmesan cheese**

1. Cook beans according to package directions.

2. Meanwhile, place the crackers and thyme in a small resealable plastic bag. Release the air from the bag and seal bag. With your hands, crush the crackers until they resemble fine crumbs. Add melted butter to the bag. Seal bag and shake to combine.

3. Place beans in a serving dish. Top with cracker mixture. Sprinkle Parmesan cheese over top. Makes 4 to 6 servings.

Per serving: 168 cal., 10 g fat (6 g sat. fat), 20 mg chol., 249 mg sodium, 13 g carbo., 2 g fiber, 4 g pro.

Quick & Cheesy Veggies

Walnuts add a nice crunch to this side dish. If some members of the family don't care for the crunchy nut topping, sprinkle it on individual servings.

Start to Finish: 10 minutes

- **1 12-ounce package frozen broccoli and cauliflower in microwavable steaming bag**
- **1 cup shredded American cheese (4 ounces)**
- **2 tablespoons chopped walnuts, toasted**

1. Cook vegetables according to package directions. Transfer vegetables to a serving bowl. Stir in cheese; let stand for 1 minute. Toss until cheese is melted and vegetables are coated. Sprinkle with nuts. Makes 4 servings.

Per serving: 158 cal., 11 g fat (6 g sat. fat), 27 mg chol., 445 mg sodium, 5 g carbo., 2 g fiber, 8 g pro.

outside the box

Sure, mac 'n' cheese is great on its own, but turn it into something that will make the family flip! Add a little love (and flavor) to your favorite packaged foods with these clever fix-ups.

Italian-Style Macaroni Salad

Prep: 20 minutes **Chill:** 10 minutes

1. Prepare one 7.25-ounce package macaroni and cheese dinner mix according to package directions, adding 1 cup frozen stir-fry pepper and onion strips during the last 2 minutes of cooking the pasta. Transfer pasta mixture to a large bowl. Cover; chill in freezer for 10 minutes, stirring once. Stir in one large seeded, chopped tomato (¾ cup) and ⅓ cup bottled Italian salad dressing. Makes 4 servings.

Per serving: 394 cal., 17 g fat (8 g sat. fat), 34 mg chol., 902 mg sodium, 49 g carbo., 2 g fiber, 11 g pro.

Here, your lunchtime go-to gets a makeover. Add zip, zing, and pizzazz to this family pantry favorite, all with the stir of a spoon. Stepping outside the box has never been easier!

Pizza-Style Mac & Cheese

Start to Finish: 25 minutes

1. Prepare one 7.25-ounce package macaroni and cheese dinner mix according to package directions. Stir in ½ cup pizza sauce. Stir in one drained 6-ounce can or jar sliced or chopped mushrooms, ¼ cup chopped pitted ripe olives, and ¼ cup chopped pepperoni; heat through, stirring occasionally. Sprinkle with grated Parmesan cheese. Makes 4 servings.

Per serving: 404 cal., 17 g fat (8 g sat. fat), 45 mg chol., 1,174 mg sodium, 49 g carbo., 2 g fiber, 14 g pro.

Mac & Cheese with Smoked Sausage

Start to Finish: 25 minutes

1. Prepare one 7.25-ounce package macaroni and cheese dinner mix according to package directions. Stir in 6 ounces cooked smoked sausage, halved lengthwise and sliced, and ¾ cup canned roasted red sweet peppers, drained and coarsely chopped. Heat through. If desired, sprinkle with snipped Italian (flat-leaf) parsley. Makes 4 servings.

Per serving: 466 cal., 24 g fat (11 g sat. fat), 58 mg chol., 965 mg sodium, 46 g carbo., 2 g fiber, 16 g pro.

Turn a plain box of rice pilaf mix into an irresistible side dish or main dish with these three sumptuous ideas. You'll have everyone in the family raving!

Autumn Vegetable Pilaf

Start to Finish: 35 minutes

1. Preheat oven to 400°F. Prepare one 6- to 7.2-ounce box rice pilaf mix according to package directions, except omit butter or oil. Stir together 2 tablespoons olive oil; 2 tablespoons cider vinegar; 2 cloves garlic, minced; and 1 teaspoon dried thyme. Add 1 sweet potato, peeled and cubed; 1 zucchini, cubed; and 1 small red onion, cut into wedges; stir to coat. Spread vegetables in a 15×10×1-inch baking pan. Roast, uncovered, 20 to 25 minutes or until vegetables are lightly browned and tender. Remove and stir into hot rice pilaf; top with ⅓ cup chopped toasted walnuts. Makes 6 servings.

Per serving: 233 cal., 9 g fat (1 g sat. fat), 0 mg chol., 328 mg sodium, 34 g carbo., 3 g fiber, 4 g pro.

Asian Chicken & Rice Salad

Start to Finish: 25 minutes

1. Prepare one 6- to 7.2-ounce box rice pilaf mix according to package directions. In a large bowl, stir together rice mix, 2 cups shredded or chopped cooked chicken, one 14-ounce can whole baby corn (drained), ½ cup chopped sweet pepper, ½ cup halved snow peas (or 1 stalk thinly sliced celery), and ¼ cup sliced green onion. Add ½ cup bottled Asian salad dressing, stirring gently to combine. Serve immediately or cover and chill for up to 24 hours. If desired, sprinkle with toasted sesame seeds before serving. Makes 4 to 6 servings.

Per serving: 429 cal., 14 g fat (3 g sat. fat), 62 mg chol., 1,057 mg sodium, 46 g carbo., 5 g fiber, 26 g pro.

Bayou Shrimp & Rice

Prep: 20 minutes **Cook:** 20 minutes

1. In a 4-quart Dutch oven, stir together one 14.5-ounce can undrained Cajun- or Mexican-style stewed tomatoes (chopped), one 14-ounce can chicken broth, 1 cup chopped onion, 1 cup chopped green sweet pepper, one 6- to 7.2-ounce box rice pilaf mix, 2 cloves garlic (minced), and 1 teaspoon Cajun seasoning. Bring to boiling; reduce heat. Cover and simmer for 20 to 25 minutes or until rice is tender and liquid is nearly absorbed. Stir occasionally. Stir in 8 ounces cooked, peeled, and deveined shrimp and 8 ounces cooked, sliced kielbasa; heat through. Makes 4 to 5 servings.

Per serving: 461 cal., 18 g fat (8 g sat. fat), 137 mg chol., 1,864 mg sodium, 49 g carbo., 3 g fiber, 25 g pro.

Skip the full-fat gravy. A bowl of mashed potatoes has tastier accompaniments with these mix-and-serve ideas.

Boursin Mashed Potatoes

Boursin is a soft triple-cream cheese seasoned with herbs and garlic. It melts to a supercreamy texture with the mashed potatoes.

Start to Finish: 10 minutes

1. Heat a 1.5-pound package refrigerated mashed potatoes according to package directions. Transfer warm potatoes to a serving bowl. Stir in one 5.2-ounce container semisoft cheese with garlic and herbs (Boursin) and 3 tablespoons snipped fresh parsley. If desired, top with canned french-fried onions. Makes 4 to 6 servings.

Per serving: 301 cal., 17 g fat (8 g sat. fat), 34 mg chol., 287 mg sodium, 27 g carbo., 1 g fiber, 7 g pro.

Bacon & Spinach Mashed Potatoes

This colorful side dish has flavors to please the whole family, and it's a good way to introduce spinach to your kids.

Start to Finish: 15 minutes

1. Heat a 1.5-pound package refrigerated mashed potatoes according to package directions. Transfer warm potatoes to a serving bowl. Stir in ¾ cup shredded cheddar cheese, 3 slices of crisp-cooked and crumbled bacon, and 2 cups of baby spinach leaves, shredded. If desired, top with additional bacon and spinach leaves. Makes 4 to 6 servings.

Per serving: 255 cal., 12 g fat (5 g sat. fat), 29 mg chol., 538 mg sodium, 24 g carbo., 2 g fiber, 12 g pro.

Pesto & Red Pepper Potatoes

Try the Homemade Pesto on page 59 in this recipe. Two frozen cubes are enough to do the trick.

Start to Finish: 10 minutes

1. Heat a 1.5-pound package refrigerated mashed potatoes according to package directions. Transfer warm potatoes to a serving bowl. Stir in ¼ cup of roasted red sweet peppers, drained and cut into strips. Gently swirl in ¼ cup purchased basil pesto or Homemade Pesto (page 59). If desired, top with ¼ cup of roasted red sweet peppers, drained and cut into strips, and shredded Parmesan cheese. Makes 4 to 6 servings.

Per serving: 268 cal., 14 g fat (1 g sat. fat), 6 mg chol., 456 mg sodium, 27 g carbo., 2 g fiber, 8 g pro.

Biscuit mix + flavor =
a rockin' good addition to mealtime.

Pesto Biscuits

Prep: 15 minutes **Bake:** 10 minutes

1. Preheat oven to 450°F. In a medium bowl, stir together $2\frac{1}{4}$ cups biscuit mix, $\frac{1}{2}$ cup milk, and $\frac{1}{4}$ cup purchased basil pesto until a soft dough forms. Turn dough out onto a lightly floured surface. Lightly knead 10 times or until nearly smooth. Pat dough to $\frac{1}{2}$ inch thick. Using a $2\frac{1}{2}$-inch round cookie cutter, cut dough into rounds. Place rounds on an ungreased baking sheet. Brush lightly with 2 teaspoons olive oil and sprinkle with 2 tablespoons finely shredded Parmesan cheese. Bake about 10 minutes or until golden. Serve warm. Makes 10 to 12 biscuits.

Per serving: 165 cal., 8 g fat (2 g sat. fat), 4 mg chol., 426 mg sodium, 19 g carbo., 1 g fiber, 4 g pro.

Blueberry-Orange Scones

Prep: 20 minutes **Bake:** 12 minutes

1. Preheat oven to 400°F. In a large bowl, stir together $2\frac{1}{4}$ cups biscuit mix, $\frac{1}{3}$ cup milk, 1 egg, and 1 teaspoon finely shredded orange peel until a soft dough forms. Carefully fold in $\frac{1}{2}$ cup fresh blueberries. Turn dough out onto a lightly floured surface. Lightly knead 10 times or until nearly smooth. Pat dough into a 6-inch circle. Cut into 6 wedges. Arrange wedges on an ungreased baking sheet. Brush with additional milk and sprinkle lightly with sugar. Bake for 12 to 14 minutes or until golden. Serve warm. Makes 6 servings.

Per serving: 230 cal., 8 g fat (2 g sat. fat), 37 mg chol., 598 mg sodium, 33 g carbo., 1 g fiber, 5 g pro.

the one-pan plan

Dinner in a flash, all in one pan—it's a busy cook's dream come true! Whether it's in a skillet, saucepan, or baking dish, all you need to do is turn on the heat. Best part? Cleanup's a breeze!

Skillet-Style Lasagna

Start to Finish: 30 minutes

- 8 ounces uncooked lean ground chicken or turkey
- ½ cup chopped onion (1 medium)
- 2 cups purchased spaghetti sauce
- 1 cup water
- 2 cups dried extra-wide noodles
- 1½ cups coarsely chopped zucchini (1 medium)
- ½ cup fat-free ricotta cheese
- 2 tablespoons grated Parmesan or Romano cheese
- 1 tablespoon snipped fresh parsley
- ½ cup shredded part-skim mozzarella cheese (2 ounces)
- Snipped fresh parsley (optional)

1. In a skillet, brown chicken and onion over medium heat; drain fat. Stir in spaghetti sauce and water. Bring to boiling; stir in uncooked noodles and zucchini. Reduce heat. Cover and simmer 10 minutes or until pasta is tender.

2. Meanwhile, in a bowl, combine ricotta cheese, Parmesan cheese, and 1 tablespoon parsley. Spoon cheese mixture onto pasta in 4 mounds. Sprinkle each with mozzarella cheese. Cover and cook over low heat 4 to 5 minutes or until mozzarella is melted. Remove from heat; let stand, uncovered, 10 minutes before serving. If desired, sprinkle with parsley. Makes 6 servings.

Per serving: 186 cal., 3 g total fat (2 g sat. fat), 45 mg chol., 519 mg sodium, 21 g carbo., 2 g fiber, 17 g pro.

One-Pot Spaghetti

Start to Finish: 40 minutes

- **8 ounces ground beef or bulk pork sausage**
- **1 cup sliced fresh mushrooms or one 6-ounce jar sliced mushrooms, drained**
- **½ cup chopped onion (1 medium)**
- **1 clove garlic, minced, or ⅛ teaspoon garlic powder**
- **1 14-ounce can chicken broth or beef broth**
- **1¾ cups water**
- **1 6-ounce can tomato paste**
- **1 teaspoon dried oregano, crushed**
- **½ teaspoon dried basil or marjoram, crushed**
- **¼ teaspoon ground black pepper**
- **6 ounces dried spaghetti, broken**
- **¼ cup grated Parmesan cheese**

1. In a large saucepan, cook the ground beef, fresh mushrooms (if using), onion, and garlic over medium heat until meat is brown and onion is tender. Drain off fat.

2. Stir in the jarred mushrooms (if using), broth, water, tomato paste, oregano, basil, and pepper. Bring to boiling. Add the broken spaghetti, a little at a time, stirring constantly. Return to boiling; reduce heat. Boil gently, uncovered, for 17 to 20 minutes or until spaghetti is tender and sauce is of the desired consistency, stirring frequently. Serve with Parmesan cheese. Makes 4 servings.

Per serving: 362 cal., 12 g fat (5 g sat. fat), 39 mg chol., 857 mg sodium, 44 g carbo., 4 g fiber, 21 g pro.

Popover Pizza Casserole

Prep: 30 minutes **Bake:** 25 minutes

- 12 ounces ground turkey or ground beef
- ¾ cup chopped onion (1 large)
- ¾ cup chopped green sweet pepper (1 medium)
- ½ of a 3.5-ounce package sliced pepperoni
- 1 14- to 15.5-ounce jar or can pizza sauce
- 1 4-ounce can mushroom stems and pieces, drained
- 1 teaspoon dried Italian seasoning, crushed
- ½ teaspoon fennel seeds, crushed
- 2 eggs
- 1 cup milk
- 1 tablespoon cooking oil
- 1 cup all-purpose flour
- 1½ cups broccoli florets
- 1 cup shredded mozzarella cheese (4 ounces)
- 2 tablespoons grated Parmesan cheese

1. In an oven-safe large skillet, cook turkey, onion, and sweet pepper over medium heat until meat is brown and vegetables are tender. Drain off fat. Halve pepperoni slices. Stir pepperoni, pizza sauce, drained mushrooms, Italian seasoning, and fennel into meat mixture. Bring to boiling; reduce heat. Simmer, uncovered, for 10 minutes; stir occasionally.

2. Preheat oven to 400°F. In a bowl, combine eggs, milk, and oil. Whisk for 1 minute. Add flour; whisk 1 minute more or until smooth. Top meat mixture in skillet with broccoli; sprinkle with mozzarella cheese. Pour milk mixture over meat mixture in skillet; cover completely. Sprinkle with Parmesan cheese. Bake, uncovered, 25 to 30 minutes or until topping is puffed and golden brown. Serve immediately. Makes 6 servings.

Per serving: 379 cal., 18 g fat (7 g sat. fat), 145 mg chol., 818 mg sodium, 29 g carbo., 3 g fiber, 24 g pro.

Hamburger-Mash Surprise

Prep: 25 minutes **Bake:** 30 minutes
Stand: 5 minutes

- ¾ **cup shredded cheddar cheese (3 ounces)**
- 2 **cups refrigerated mashed potatoes**
- 12 **ounces lean ground beef**
- ½ **cup chopped onion**
- 2 **cups sliced zucchini or yellow summer squash**
- 1 **14½-ounce can diced tomatoes with basil, oregano, and garlic, undrained**
- ½ **of a 6-ounce can (⅓ cup) no-sodium tomato paste**
- ¼ **teaspoon ground black pepper**
- **Paprika (optional)**

1. Preheat oven to 375°F. Stir ½ cup of the cheese into the potatoes; set aside. In a large oven-safe skillet,* cook ground beef and onion until meat is no longer pink and onion is tender. Drain off fat. Stir in squash, undrained tomatoes, tomato paste, and pepper. Bring to boiling. Remove from heat.

2. Spoon mashed potato mixture into a large reasealable plastic bag. Seal bag; snip off a corner of the plastic bag. Starting at one end of the skillet, pipe the potato mixture in rows across the top of meat mixture until meat mixture is covered. (Or spoon mashed potato mixture in mounds on top of hot mixture.) Sprinkle with remaining ¼ cup cheese. If desired, sprinkle potato mixture with paprika.

3. Bake, uncovered, for 30 minutes or until mashed potato top is golden brown. Let stand 5 minutes before serving. Makes 6 servings.

***Tip:** If you don't own an oven-safe skillet, transfer beef-vegetable mixture to a 2-quart casserole dish at the end of step 1. Continue as directed.

Per serving: 284 cal., 14 g fat (6 g sat. fat), 53 mg chol., 602 mg sodium, 21 g carbo., 2 g fiber, 18 g pro.

Crunchy Beef Wraps

Beef, cabbage, and corn come together in a savory saucy mixture that is wrapped up in hot tortillas and ready to go! Perfect for lunch, dinner, or a little something in between.

Start to Finish: 20 minutes

- 8 8-inch flour tortillas
- ¾ pound lean ground beef
- ½ cup chopped red or green onion
- 2 cups packaged shredded cabbage with carrot (coleslaw mix)
- 1 cup frozen whole kernel corn
- ¼ cup bottled barbecue sauce
- 1 teaspoon toasted sesame oil
- Barbecue sauce (optional)

1. Preheat oven to 350°F. Stack tortillas and wrap in foil. Heat in the oven for 10 minutes. Meanwhile, in a large skillet, cook ground beef and onion over medium heat until meat is brown. Drain well. Stir in cabbage mix and corn. Cover; cook about 4 minutes or until vegetables are tender, stirring once. Stir in barbecue sauce and sesame oil. Cook and stir until heated through.

2. Spoon ½ cup filling onto each tortilla below center. Fold bottom edge up and over filling. Fold opposite sides in, just until they meet. Roll up from bottom. If desired, serve with additional barbecue sauce. Makes 4 servings (2 wraps each).

Per serving: 388 cal., 14 g total fat (5 g sat. fat), 54 mg chol., 409 mg sodium, 44 g carbo., 4 g fiber, 21 g pro.

Steak & Mushrooms

Start to Finish: 30 minutes

- 4 **beef tenderloin steaks, cut 1 inch thick (about 1 pound)**
- **Salt and ground black pepper**
- 1 **tablespoon olive oil**
- 1 **tablespoon bottled minced garlic**
- ½ **cup chopped red onion**
- 1 **medium green sweet pepper, cut into thin strips**
- 1 **8-ounce package presliced button mushrooms (3 cups)**
- ¼ **cup onion-flavor beef broth or beef broth**
- ¼ **cup whipping cream**

1. Season meat lightly with salt and black pepper. In a large skillet, heat oil over medium-high heat until very hot. Add meat. Reduce heat to medium and cook for 10 to 13 minutes or to desired doneness, turning once. Transfer steaks to a serving platter; keep warm.

2. In the same skillet, cook and stir garlic, onion, sweet pepper, and mushrooms over medium-high heat about 6 minutes or until tender and most of the liquid has evaporated. Stir in broth and cream. Bring to boiling. Boil gently, uncovered, over medium heat about 4 minutes or until slightly thickened, stirring occasionally. Spoon mushroom mixture over steaks. Makes 4 servings.

Per serving: 298 cal., 18 g fat (7 g sat. fat), 90 mg chol., 191 mg sodium, 7 g carbo., 1 g fiber, 26 g pro.

Garlic-Mustard Steak Sandwiches

Prep: 15 minutes **Broil:** 13 minutes

- **4 to 6 hoagie rolls, split**
- **2 tablespoons honey mustard**
- **½ teaspoon dried thyme, crushed**
- **1 clove garlic, minced**
- **¼ teaspoon coarsely ground black pepper**
- **1 to 1½ pounds beef flank steak**
- **1 large red onion, sliced ½ inch thick**
- **4 to 6 slices Swiss cheese**
- **Honey mustard (optional)**

1. Preheat broiler. Place rolls, cut sides up, on a broiler pan. Broil 4 to 5 inches from heat for 1 to 2 minutes or until toasted. Set aside. In a bowl, mix mustard, thyme, garlic, and pepper.

2. Trim fat from steak. Score steak on both sides by making shallow diagonal cuts at 1-inch intervals in a diamond pattern. Brush both sides of steak with mustard mixture.

3. Place steak on broiler pan. Place onion slices beside steak. Broil 4 to 5 inches from heat for 12 to 17 minutes or until steak is desired doneness and onion is tender, turning steak and onion slices once.

4. Thinly slice steak at an angle across the grain. Separate onion slices into rings. Arrange steak strips, onion rings, and cheese on roll bottoms. Broil 1 minute or until cheese starts to melt. Add roll tops. If desired, pass additional mustard at the table. Makes 4 to 6 servings.

Per serving: 685 cal., 22 g fat (9 g sat. fat), 65 mg chol., 844 mg sodium, 78 g carbo., 4 g fiber, 43 g pro.

Microwave Meat Loaf with Tomato Sauce

Start to Finish: 40 minutes

- 1 **8-ounce can pizza sauce**
- ½ **cup shredded zucchini**
- ¼ **cup rolled oats**
- ¼ **cup finely chopped onion**
- 3 **tablespoons snipped fresh parsley**
- 1 **teaspoon bottled minced garlic**
- 1 **teaspoon dried thyme, crushed**
- ¼ **teaspoon salt**
- ¼ **teaspoon ground black pepper**
- 1 **pound lean ground beef**
- ½ **pound uncooked ground turkey breast**

1. In a bowl, combine 2 tablespoons of the pizza sauce, the zucchini, oats, onion, 2 tablespoons of the parsley, ½ teaspoon of the garlic, the thyme, salt, and pepper. Add beef and turkey; mix well. Shape meat mixture into a 7×4×2-inch loaf. Place loaf in a greased 9-inch microwave-safe pie plate or greased 2-quart square baking dish.

2. Cover meat loaf with waxed paper. Microwave on 100-percent power (high) for 5 minutes, turning plate once (if your microwave has a turntable, there is no need to turn the dish). Tilt dish slightly and spoon off drippings. In a small bowl, stir together the remaining pizza sauce, remaining 1 tablespoon parsley, and remaining ½ teaspoon garlic. Pour evenly over meat loaf. Cover with waxed paper; microwave on 50-percent power (medium) for 21 to 24 minutes or until cooked through (165°F), turning plate twice. Makes 6 servings.

Per serving: 243 cal., 12 g fat (5 g sat. fat), 66 mg chol., 380 mg sodium, 7 g carbo., 1 g fiber, 24 g pro.

Spiced Meatball Stew

Start to Finish: 30 minutes

- 1 16-ounce package frozen prepared Italian-style meatballs
- 3 cups green beans, cut into 1-inch pieces, or frozen cut green beans
- 2 cups peeled baby carrots
- 1 $14\frac{1}{2}$-ounce can beef broth
- 2 teaspoons Worcestershire sauce
- ½ to ¾ teaspoon ground allspice
- 1 piece (1-inch) stick cinnamon
- 2 14.5-ounce cans stewed tomatoes, undrained

1. In a Dutch oven, combine meatballs, green beans, carrots, beef broth, Worcestershire sauce, allspice, and cinnamon. Bring to boiling; reduce heat. Cover and simmer for 10 minutes. Stir in undrained tomatoes. Return to boiling; reduce heat. Cover; simmer 5 minutes more or until vegetables are tender. Remove cinnamon stick.

To Make Ahead: Prepare as directed. Freeze stew in an airtight freezer container. To reheat, place frozen stew in a large saucepan. Heat, covered, over medium heat about 30 minutes, stirring occasionally to break apart. Makes 10 cups.

Per serving: 233 cal., 13 g fat (6 g sat. fat), 37 mg chol., 938 mg sodium, 18 g carbo., 4 g fiber, 12 g pro.

Peppered Pork Chops & Pilaf

For a speedier supper, pick up assorted cut-up vegetables from the salad bar at your local supermarket.

Start to Finish: 25 minutes

- **4 3-ounce boneless pork loin chops, cut ¾ inch thick**
- **2 teaspoons seasoned pepper blend**
- **1 tablespoon olive oil**
- **3 cups vegetables, such as broccoli, carrots, onions, and/or sweet peppers, cut into bite-size pieces**
- **1 14-ounce can chicken broth**
- **2 cups uncooked instant brown rice**
- **¼ cup roasted red sweet pepper strips**

1. Sprinkle both sides of chops with the seasoned pepper blend. In a large skillet, cook chops in hot oil over medium heat for 5 minutes. Turn chops. Cook for 3 to 7 minutes more or until slightly pink in the center and juices run clear (160°F). Remove chops from skillet; cover and keep warm.

2. Add vegetables, broth, and rice to skillet. Bring to boiling; reduce heat. Cover and simmer for 5 to 7 minutes or until rice is tender and vegetables are crisp-tender. Return pork chops to skillet; cover and heat through. Garnish with roasted red pepper strips. Makes 4 servings.

Per serving: 305 cal., 9 g fat (2 g sat. fat), 47 mg chol., 606 mg sodium, 32 g carbo., 4 g fiber, 24 g pro.

Glazed Teriyaki Pork Chops with Potatoes

Prep: 20 minutes **Broil:** 9 minutes

- 4 **boneless pork loin chops, cut ¾ inch thick**
- ¼ **cup bottled teriyaki glaze**
- 12 **ounces tiny new potatoes, quartered**
- 1 **tablespoon olive oil**
- 1 **tablespoon toasted sesame oil**
- ¼ **teaspoon salt**
- ⅛ **teaspoon ground black pepper**
- 1 **cup pea pods, halved lengthwise**
- **Bottled teriyaki glaze (optional)**

1. Preheat broiler. Brush both sides of chops with the ¼ cup teriyaki glaze. Arrange chops on half of the broiler pan; set aside.

2. In a large bowl, toss potatoes with olive oil, sesame oil, salt, and pepper until coated. Arrange potatoes in a single layer next to chops.

3. Broil 4 inches from heat for 9 to 11 minutes or until pork is done (160°F) and potatoes are tender, turning pork and potatoes once.

4. Place pea pods in a large bowl. Add potatoes and toss to combine. Serve pork with potatoes and pea pods. If desired, pass additional teriyaki glaze. Makes 4 servings.

Per serving: 394 cal., 15 g fat (4 g sat. fat), 86 mg chol., 626 mg sodium, 23 g carbo., 2 g fiber, 38 g pro.

Oriental Pork & Vegetables

Prep: 10 minutes **Cook:** 8 minutes

- 6 **ounces wide rice noodles or rice stick noodles, broken if desired**
- 2 **teaspoons sesame oil or olive oil**
- 1 **16-ounce package frozen stir-fry vegetables**
- 1 **12-ounce pork tenderloin, cut into ¼-inch-thick slices**
- ¼ **cup bottled teriyaki sauce**
- 2 **tablespoons plum sauce**

1. Discard spice packet from ramen noodles, if using, or save for another use. Prepare noodles as directed on package. Set aside and keep warm.

2. Heat 12-inch nonstick skillet over medium-high heat. Add 1 teaspoon of the sesame oil. Cook and stir vegetables for 4 to 6 minutes or until crisp-tender. Remove vegetables from skillet. Set aside and keep warm.

3. Add remaining 1 teaspoon oil to skillet. Add pork and cook over medium-high heat for 4 to 6 minutes or until no longer pink, turning slices once. Stir in vegetables (drained if necessary), teriyaki sauce, and plum sauce; heat through. Toss pork mixture with noodles. Makes 4 servings.

Note: Find bottled teriyaki and plum sauces in the Asian aisle of your supermarket.

Per serving: 341 cal., 5 g fat (1 g sat. fat), 55 mg chol., 820 mg sodium, 48 g carbo., 3 g fiber, 22 g pro.

Vermicelli with Sausage & Spinach

Start to Finish: 25 minutes

- 1 pound cooked smoked sausage, halved lengthwise and cut into ½-inch-thick slices
- ¾ cup chopped onion (1 large)
- 2 large cloves garlic, chopped
- 2 teaspoons olive oil
- 2 14-ounce cans reduced-sodium chicken broth
- ¼ cup water
- 8 ounces dried vermicelli or angel hair pasta, broken in half
- 1 9-ounce package fresh prewashed baby spinach
- ¼ teaspoon freshly ground black pepper
- ⅓ cup whipping cream

1. In a 4-quart Dutch oven, cook sausage, onion, and garlic in hot oil over medium-high heat until onion is tender and sausage is lightly browned.

2. Add broth and the water; bring to boiling. Add pasta; cook for 3 minutes, stirring frequently. Add spinach and pepper; cook about 1 minute more or until spinach is wilted. Stir in cream. Serve immediately. Makes 4 to 6 servings.

Per serving: 782 cal., 47 g fat (18 g sat. fat), 104 mg chol., 2,556 mg sodium, 52 g carbo., 4 g fiber, 38 g pro.

Rotini-Kielbasa Skillet

Start to Finish: 35 minutes

- 2 cups dried rotini pasta (about 6 ounces)
- 1 tablespoon olive oil
- 1 medium onion, cut into wedges
- 2 cloves garlic, minced
- 1 pound cooked turkey kielbasa, halved lengthwise and sliced diagonally
- 1 small zucchini, coarsely chopped
- 1 yellow or orange sweet pepper, cut into small strips
- 1 teaspoon dried Italian seasoning, crushed
- ⅛ teaspoon cayenne pepper
- 8 roma tomatoes, cored and chopped (about 1 pound)

1. Cook pasta according to package directions; drain. Meanwhile, in a large skillet, heat oil over medium-high heat. Add onion and garlic; cook for 1 minute. Add kielbasa; cook and stir until onion is tender.

2. Add zucchini, sweet pepper, Italian seasoning, and cayenne pepper; cook and stir for 5 minutes. Stir in tomatoes and pasta. Heat through. Makes 6 servings.

Per serving: 267 cal., 10 g fat (2 g sat. fat), 47 mg chol., 677 mg sodium, 29 g carbo., 2 g fiber, 15 g pro.

Greek Skillet Supper

Prep: 20 minutes **Cook:** 15 minutes

- 8 ounces lean ground lamb or ground beef
- ¾ cup chopped onion (1 large)
- 2 cloves garlic, minced
- 1 14½-ounce can beef broth
- 1½ cups dried medium shell macaroni
- 2 cups frozen mixed vegetables
- 1 14.5-ounce can tomatoes, undrained and cut up
- 2 tablespoons tomato paste
- ⅛ teaspoon ground cinnamon
- ⅛ teaspoon ground nutmeg
- 2 teaspoons snipped fresh marjoram
- ½ cup crumbled feta cheese (2 ounces)

1. In a large skillet, cook meat, onion, and garlic over medium heat until meat is brown and onion is tender. Drain off fat. Stir in broth and macaroni. Bring to boiling; reduce heat. Cover; simmer for 10 minutes.

2. Stir in vegetables, undrained tomatoes, tomato paste, cinnamon, and nutmeg. Return to boiling; reduce heat. Simmer, uncovered, 5 to 10 minutes or until vegetables are tender. Stir in marjoram. Sprinkle with feta and, if desired, additional marjoram. Makes 4 servings.

Per serving: 400 cal., 12 g fat (6 g sat. fat), 50 mg chol., 783 mg sodium, 51 g carbo., 3 g fiber, 22 g pro.

Pesto Chicken Breasts with Veggies

Prep: 15 minutes **Broil:** 11 minutes

- 4 **medium skinless, boneless chicken breast halves (about 1½ pounds)**
- ¼ **cup purchased basil pesto or Homemade Pesto (page 59)**
- 1 **medium zucchini or yellow summer squash**
- 3 **tablespoons olive oil**
- ¼ **teaspoon salt**
- ⅛ **teaspoon ground black pepper**
- 1 **8-ounce loaf or half of a 16-ounce loaf Italian bread, halved lengthwise**
- 2 **tablespoons grated Parmesan cheese**

1. Preheat broiler. Brush both sides of chicken with pesto; arrange chicken on one end of a broiler pan. Broil 4 inches from heat for 5 minutes. Remove pan and turn chicken.

2. Meanwhile, cut zucchini lengthwise into ¼-inch-thick slices. Brush slices with 1½ tablespoons of the olive oil and sprinkle with salt and pepper. Arrange zucchini on pan next to chicken.

3. Broil for 5 to 8 minutes more or until chicken is done (170°F) and zucchini is tender, turning zucchini once. Transfer chicken and zucchini to a serving platter; cover to keep warm.

4. Brush cut sides of bread with the remaining 1½ tablespoons olive oil. Sprinkle with Parmesan. Place bread, cut sides up, on broiler pan. Broil 4 inches from heat for 1 to 2 minutes or until toasted. Cut bread crosswise into slices and serve with chicken and zucchini. Makes 4 servings.

Per serving: 531 cal., 25 g fat (3 g sat. fat), 86 mg chol., 713 mg sodium, 33 g carbo., 2 g fiber, 41 g pro.

Greek-Style Chicken Skillet

To add even more interest to this dish, choose a flavored couscous mix in place of the plain couscous.

Start to Finish: 40 minutes

- **4 skinless, boneless chicken breast halves (about 1¼ pounds total)**
- **Salt and ground black pepper**
- **1 tablespoon olive oil or cooking oil**
- **1½ cups sliced zucchini (1 medium)**
- **¾ cup chopped green sweet pepper (1 medium)**
- **1 medium onion, sliced and separated into rings**
- **2 cloves garlic, minced**
- **⅛ teaspoon ground black pepper**
- **¼ cup water**
- **1 10.75-ounce can condensed tomato soup**
- **2 cups hot cooked couscous or small pasta (orzo)**
- **½ cup crumbled feta cheese (2 ounces)**
- **Lemon wedges**

1. Season chicken with salt and black pepper to taste. In a large skillet, cook chicken in hot oil over medium heat for 12 to 15 minutes or until no longer pink (170°F), turning once. Remove chicken from skillet; keep warm.

2. Add zucchini, sweet pepper, onion, garlic, and black pepper to skillet. Add the water; reduce heat. Cover and cook for 5 minutes, stirring once or twice. Stir in soup. Bring to boiling; reduce heat. Cover and simmer for 5 minutes more, stirring once.

3. Return chicken to skillet, turning to coat. Serve with couscous, feta, and lemon wedges. Makes 4 servings.

Per serving: 401 cal., 10 g fat (4 g sat. fat), 99 mg chol., 827 mg sodium, 36 g carbo., 4 g fiber, 41 g pro.

Zesty Chicken with Black Beans & Rice

Start to Finish: 30 minutes

- **1 pound skinless, boneless chicken breast halves, cut into 2-inch pieces**
- **2 tablespoons cooking oil**
- **1 6- to 7.4-ounce package Spanish rice pilaf mix**
- **1¾ cups water**
- **1 15-ounce can black beans, rinsed and drained**
- **1 14½-ounce can diced tomatoes, undrained**
- **Sour cream, sliced green onion, and lime wedges (optional)**

1. In a large skillet, brown the chicken pieces in 1 tablespoon of the oil over medium heat. Remove from skillet; keep warm.

2. Add rice mix and remaining 1 tablespoon oil to skillet; cook and stir for 2 minutes. Stir in seasoning packet from rice mix, the water, drained beans, and undrained tomatoes; add chicken. Bring to boiling; reduce heat. Cover; simmer about 20 minutes or until rice is tender. If desired, serve with sour cream, green onion, and lime wedges. Makes 4 servings.

Per serving: 424 cal., 9 g fat (2 g sat. fat), 66 mg chol., 1,080 mg sodium, 52 g carbo., 6 g fiber, 37 g pro.

Shrimp and Couscous Jambalaya

Start to Finish: 25 minutes

- **12 ounces fresh medium shrimp, peeled and deveined**
- **1 cup sliced celery (2 stalks)**
- **¾ cup chopped green sweet pepper (1 medium)**
- **½ cup chopped onion (1 medium)**
- **½ teaspoon Cajun seasoning**
- **¼ teaspoon dried oregano, crushed**
- **2 tablespoons cooking oil**
- **1 14-ounce can reduced-sodium chicken broth**
- **1 cup quick-cooking couscous**
- **½ cup chopped tomato (1 medium)**
- **Bottled hot pepper sauce and lemon wedges (optional)**

1. Rinse shrimp and pat dry; set aside. In a large skillet, cook celery, sweet pepper, onion, Cajun seasoning, and oregano in oil over medium heat until tender. Add broth; bring to boiling. Stir in shrimp; remove from heat. Stir in couscous and tomato. Cover; let stand 5 minutes. If desired, serve with hot pepper sauce and lemon. Makes 4 servings.

Per serving: 317 cal., 8 g fat (1 g sat. fat), 98 mg chol., 462 mg sodium, 42 g carbo., 9 g fiber, 18 g pro.

Dilled Shrimp with Rice

Start to Finish: 25 minutes

- 1 **tablespoon butter**
- 1½ **cups shredded carrot (3 medium)**
- 1 **cup sugar snap peas**
- ⅓ **cup sliced green onion (3)**
- 1 **pound cooked, peeled, and deveined shrimp**
- 2 **cups cooked rice**
- 1 **teaspoon finely shredded lemon peel**
- ¾ **cup chicken or vegetable broth**
- 1 **tablespoon snipped fresh dill or ½ teaspoon dried dillweed**

1. In a large skillet, melt butter over medium heat. Add carrot, peas, and onion; cook and stir 2 to 3 minutes or until vegetables are crisp-tender.

2. Stir shrimp, rice, lemon peel, and broth into skillet; heat through. Stir in dill. Makes 4 servings.

Per serving: 291 cal., 5 g fat (2 g sat. fat), 230 mg chol., 495 mg sodium, 32 g carbo., 3 g fiber, 26 g pro.

Salmon with Tropical Rice

Prep: 15 minutes **Bake:** 15 minutes

- 1 1½-pound fresh or frozen skinless salmon fillet, 1 inch thick
- 2 teaspoons olive oil
- 1 teaspoon lemon-pepper seasoning
- 1 8.8-ounce pouch cooked brown or white rice
- 1 medium mango, peeled, seeded, and chopped
- 1 tablespoon snipped fresh cilantro
- 1 teaspoon finely shredded lemon peel
- Lemon wedges (optional)
- Fresh cilantro sprigs (optional)

1. Preheat oven to 450°F. Thaw salmon, if frozen. Rinse fish and pat dry with paper towels. Place fish in a greased 3-quart rectangular baking dish. Drizzle olive oil over fish. Sprinkle with lemon-pepper seasoning.

2. In a medium bowl, stir together rice, mango, snipped cilantro, and lemon peel, breaking up rice with a spoon. Spoon rice mixture around fish. Bake, uncovered, for 15 minutes or until fish flakes easily when tested with a fork.

3. To serve, cut fish into 4 serving-size pieces. Serve fish on top of rice mixture. If desired, garnish each serving with lemon wedges and cilantro sprigs. Makes 4 servings.

Per serving: 462 cal., 22 g fat (4 g sat. fat), 99 mg chol., 104 mg sodium, 27 g carbo., 2 g fiber, 36 g pro.

Lemony Cod with Asparagus

Cod is a mild-flavored lean white fish. It is versatile in cooking and can be found either fresh or frozen in most supermarkets.

Prep: 10 minutes **Broil:** 5 minutes

- **4 purchased soft breadsticks**
- **2 tablespoons butter, melted**
- **¼ teaspoon garlic salt**
- **1 pound fresh or frozen cod fillets (½ inch thick)**
- **12 ounces asparagus spears, trimmed**
- **1 tablespoon lemon juice**
- **½ teaspoon dried thyme, crushed**
- **⅛ teaspoon ground black pepper**
- **Lemon wedges (optional)**

1. Preheat broiler. Place breadsticks on broiler pan. Brush with 1 tablespoon of the melted butter and sprinkle with garlic salt. Broil 4 inches from heat for 1 to 2 minutes or until golden, turning once. Remove from pan and keep warm.

2. Arrange fish and asparagus in a single layer on the broiler pan. In a small bowl, stir together the remaining 1 tablespoon butter and lemon juice. Drizzle butter mixture over fish and brush over asparagus. Sprinkle fish and asparagus with thyme and pepper.

3. Broil 4 inches from heat for 4 to 6 minutes or until fish flakes easily when tested with a fork and asparagus is crisp-tender; turn asparagus once. Serve with breadsticks and, if desired, lemon wedges. Makes 4 servings.

Per serving: 293 cal., 8 g fat (4 g sat. fat), 64 mg chol., 454 mg sodium, 29 g carbo., 3 g fiber, 27 g pro.

Broiled Rice & Tuna Patties

Start to Finish: 30 minutes

- **1 6-ounce can tuna, drained and flaked**
- **½ of an 8.8-ounce package cooked whole grain brown rice (1 cup)**
- **½ cup finely shredded carrot (1 medium)**
- **⅓ cup finely chopped onion (1 small)**
- **⅓ cup chopped dry-roasted peanuts**
- **¼ cup fine dry bread crumbs**
- **1 tablespoon snipped fresh parsley**
- **1 tablespoon milk**
- **½ teaspoon dried dillweed**
- **⅛ teaspoon ground black pepper**
- **1 egg, lightly beaten**
- **Nonstick cooking spray**
- **2 English muffins, split**
- **4 ounces American cheese, sliced**
- **Pickle slices**

1. Preheat broiler. In a large bowl, stir together tuna, rice, carrot, onion, peanuts, bread crumbs, parsley, milk, dillweed, and pepper. Add egg and mix well.

2. Shape mixture into four ¾-inch-thick patties. Lightly coat broiler pan with cooking spray and place patties on pan.

3. Broil 4 inches from the heat for 7 minutes. Turn patties over; add English muffin halves to rack. Broil about 2 minutes more or until patties are cooked through (160°F) and muffins are toasted.

4. Place a tuna patty on each muffin half. Top evenly with cheese. Broil for 1 to 2 minutes more or until cheese melts. Serve with pickle slices. Makes 4 servings.

Per serving: 147 cal., 5 g fat (2 g sat. fat), 22 mg chol., 265 mg sodium, 18 g carbo., 1 g fiber, 7 g pro.

A-to-Z Vegetable Soup

Start to Finish: 45 minutes

- **2 cups cut-up mixed fresh vegetables, such as zucchini, carrot, broccoli, and/or red sweet pepper**
- **1 tablespoon cooking oil or olive oil**
- **2 14-ounce cans reduced-sodium chicken broth**
- **2 cloves garlic, minced**
- **1 15-ounce can cannellini or Great Northern beans, rinsed and drained**
- **½ cup dried alphabet-shape pasta or tiny shells**
- **2 tablespoons fresh oregano leaves or 1 teaspoon dried oregano, crushed**

1. In a large saucepan, cook vegetables in hot oil over medium-high heat about 5 minutes or until crisp-tender.

2. Add broth and garlic to vegetables in saucepan. Bring to boiling. Stir in drained beans, pasta, and dried oregano, if using. Return to boiling; reduce heat. Cover and simmer about 10 minutes or until pasta is just tender. Stir in fresh oregano leaves, if using. Makes 4 servings.

Per serving: 188 cal., 4 g fat (1 g sat. fat), 0 mg chol., 717 mg sodium, 33 g carbo., 6 g fiber, 12 g pro.

forget about it!

Your very own personal chef is ready and waiting inside the cupboard: your slow cooker. Simply toss in a few ingredients and turn the dial on your way out the door. When you return ... dinner's done!

Finger Lickin' BBQ Chicken

Prep: 10 minutes
Cook: 7 hours (low) or 3½ hours (high)
Slow cooker size: 3½- or 4-quart

- **2½ to 3 pounds chicken drumsticks, skinned, if desired**
- **1 cup bottled barbecue sauce**
- **⅓ cup apricot or peach preserves**
- **2 teaspoons yellow mustard**

1. Place chicken in a 3½- or 4-quart slow cooker. In a bowl, combine barbecue sauce, preserves, and mustard. Pour over chicken.

2. Cover; cook on low-heat setting for 7 to 8 hours or on high-heat setting for 3½ to 4 hours. Remove chicken to platter; cover. Transfer sauce mixture in cooker to a medium saucepan. Bring to boiling; reduce heat. Simmer, uncovered, for 10 minutes or until desired consistency. Serve sauce with chicken. Makes 4 to 6 servings.

Per serving: 456 cal., 17 g fat (4 g sat. fat), 154 mg chol., 963 mg sodium, 37 g carbo., 2 g fiber, 38 g pro.

Ginger Chicken

Prep: 20 minutes
Cook: 5 hours (low) or 2½ hours (high)
Slow cooker size: 4- or 5-quart

- **½ cup mango chutney**
- **¼ cup bottled chili sauce**
- **2 tablespoons quick-cooking tapioca**
- **1½ teaspoons grated fresh ginger or ½ teaspoon ground ginger**
- **12 chicken thighs, skinned (about 4 pounds)**
- **Hot cooked brown rice (optional)**
- **Sliced green onion (optional)**

1. Using kitchen scissors, snip any large pieces of fruit in the chutney. In a 4- or 5-quart slow cooker, combine chutney, chili sauce, tapioca, and ginger. Add chicken, turning to coat.

2. Cover and cook on low-heat setting for 5 to 6 hours or on high-heat setting for 2½ to 3 hours. If desired, serve chicken over rice and sprinkle with green onion. Makes 6 servings.

Per serving: 264 cal., 7 g fat (2 g sat. fat), 143 mg chol., 494 mg sodium, 16 g carbo., 1 g fiber, 34 g pro.

Chicken & Noodles with Vegetables

Prep: 25 minutes
Cook: 8 hours (low) or 4 hours (high)
Slow cooker size: 3½ or 4-quart

- 2 cups sliced carrot (4 medium)
- 1½ cups chopped onion (3 medium)
- 1 cup sliced celery (2 stalks)
- 2 tablespoons snipped fresh parsley
- 1 bay leaf
- 3 medium chicken legs (drumstick-thigh portion) (about 2 pounds total), skinned
- 2 10.75-ounce cans reduced-fat and reduced-sodium condensed cream of chicken soup
- 1 teaspoon dried thyme, crushed
- 10 ounces dried wide noodles (about 5 cups)
- 1 cup frozen peas

1. In a 3½- or 4-quart slow cooker, stir together carrot, onion, celery, parsley, and bay leaf. Place chicken on top of vegetables. In a bowl, stir together soup, ½ cup *water*, thyme, and ¼ teaspoon *ground black pepper*. Pour over chicken in the slow cooker.

2. Cover and cook on low-heat setting for 8 to 9 hours or on high-heat setting for 4 to 4½ hours. Remove chicken from slow cooker; cool slightly. Discard bay leaf.

3. Cook noodles according to package directions; drain. Remove chicken from bones and shred or chop; discard bones. Stir chicken and peas into mixture in slow cooker. To serve, spoon over noodles. Makes 6 servings.

Per serving: 406 cal., 7 g fat (2 g sat. fat), 122 mg chol., 532 mg sodium, 56 g carbo., 5 g fiber, 26 g pro.

Chicken Curry Soup

Prep: 15 minutes **Cook:** 4 hours (low) or 2 hours (high) + 15 minutes (low)
Slow cooker size: 3½- or 4-quart

- 1 10¾-ounce can condensed cream of chicken soup
- 1 cup water
- 2 teaspoons curry powder
- 1¼ pounds skinless, boneless chicken thighs or breast halves, cut into ¾-inch pieces
- 2 cups sliced carrot (4 medium)
- 1 13½-ounce can unsweetened coconut milk
- 1 red sweet pepper, cut into thin, bite-size strips
- ½ cup sliced green onion (4)
- Chopped peanuts and/or toasted coconut (optional)

1. In a 3½- or 4-quart slow cooker, combine soup and water. Stir in curry powder. Add the chicken and carrot to cooker. Stir to mix.

2. Cover and cook on low-heat setting for 4 to 5 hours or on high-heat setting for 2 to 2½ hours. If using high-heat setting, turn to low. Stir in coconut milk, sweet pepper, and green onion. Cover and cook for 15 minutes more. If desired, garnish with peanuts and/or toasted coconut. Makes about 8 cups.

Per 1½ cups: 309 cal., 19 g fat (12 g sat. fat), 80 mg chol., 479 mg sodium, 13 g carbo., 2 g fiber, 22 g pro.

Southwestern White Chili

Prep: 20 minutes
Cook: 8 hours (low) or 4 hours (high)
Slow cooker size: 3½- to 5-quart

- **3 15½-ounce cans Great Northern beans, drained and rinsed**
- **4 cups reduced-sodium chicken broth**
- **3 cups chopped cooked chicken**
- **2 4-ounce cans diced green chile pepper**
- **1 cup chopped onion (2 medium)**
- **4 cloves garlic, minced**
- **2 teaspoons ground cumin**
- **1 teaspoon dried oregano, crushed**
- **¼ teaspoon cayenne pepper**
- **2 cups shredded Monterey Jack cheese (8 ounces)**
- **Sour cream (optional)**
- **Fresh cilantro leaves (optional)**

1. In a 3½- to 5-quart slow cooker, place beans, broth, chicken, chile pepper, onion, garlic, cumin, oregano, and cayenne. Stir to combine.

2. Cover and cook on low-heat setting for 8 to 10 hours or on high-heat setting for 4 to 5 hours. Stir in the cheese until melted. If desired, top servings with sour cream and cilantro. Makes 8 servings.

Per serving: 429 cal., 14 g total fat (7 g sat. fat), 72 mg chol., 570 mg sodium, 41 g carbo., 9 g fiber, 37 g pro.

Sausage-Corn Chowder

Prep: 15 minutes
Cook: 8 hours (low) or 4 hours (high)
Slow cooker size: 3½- to 5-quart

- 12 ounces cooked smoked turkey sausage, halved lengthwise and cut into ½-inch slices
- 3 cups frozen loose-pack diced hash brown potatoes with onions and peppers
- 2 medium carrots, coarsely chopped
- 2½ cups water
- 1 15- to 16½-ounce can no-salt cream-style corn
- 1 10¾-ounce can condensed golden mushroom soup
- ½ cup roasted red sweet pepper strips
- 1 teaspoon dried thyme, crushed

1. In a 3½- to 5-quart slow cooker, place sausage, frozen potatoes, and carrot. In a large bowl, stir together water, corn, soup, red pepper strips, and thyme. Add to cooker; stir to combine.

2. Cover and cook on low-heat setting for 8 to 10 hours or on high-heat setting for 4 to 5 hours. Makes 6 servings.

Per serving: 258 cal., 7 g total fat (2 g sat. fat), 40 mg chol., 893 mg sodium, 37 g carbo., 4 g fiber, 13 g pro.

Turkey & Wild Rice Amandine

Prep: 15 minutes
Cook: 6 hours (low) or 3 hours (high)
Slow cooker size: 4- or 5-quart

- **1 6-ounce jar whole mushrooms, drained**
- **1 10.75-ounce can condensed cream of mushroom with roasted garlic soup**
- **1 8-ounce can sliced water chestnuts, drained**
- **1 cup wild rice, rinsed and drained**
- **1 cup brown rice**
- **½ cup chopped onion (1 medium)**
- **¼ teaspoon ground black pepper**
- **3 14-ounce cans reduced-sodium chicken broth**
- **3 cups shredded cooked turkey or chicken (about 1 pound)**
- **1 cup dairy sour cream**
- **½ cup sliced almonds, toasted**

1. In a 4- or 5-quart slow cooker, stir together drained mushrooms, soup, water chestnuts, uncooked wild rice, uncooked brown rice, onion, and ground black pepper. Stir in broth and ½ cup *water.*

2. Cover and cook on low-heat setting for 6 to 7 hours or on high-heat setting for 3 to 3½ hours. Stir in turkey. Top servings with sour cream and toasted almonds. Makes 10 servings.

Per serving: 340 cal., 12 g fat (4 g sat. fat), 42 mg chol., 604 mg sodium, 40 g carbo., 3 g fiber, 21 g pro.

Salsa Swiss Steak

Prep: 20 minutes
Cook: 9 hours (low) or 4½ hours (high)
Slow cooker size: 3½- or 4-quart

- **2 pounds boneless beef round steak, cut 1 inch thick**
- **1 to 2 large red or green sweet peppers, cut into bite-size strips**
- **1 medium onion, sliced**
- **1 10.75-ounce can condensed cream of mushroom soup**
- **1 cup bottled salsa**
- **2 tablespoons all-purpose flour**
- **1 teaspoon dry mustard**

1. Trim fat from meat. Cut meat into 6 serving-size pieces. In a 3½- or 4-quart slow cooker, place meat, sweet pepper, and onion. In a medium bowl, stir together soup, salsa, flour, and mustard. Pour into slow cooker.

2. Cover and cook on low-heat setting for 9 to 10 hours or on high-heat setting for 4½ to 5 hours. Makes 6 servings.

Per serving: 251 cal., 6 g fat (2 g sat. fat), 65 mg chol., 574 mg sodium, 10 g carbo., 1 g fiber, 37 g pro.

Greek-Style Beef & Vegetables

Prep: 15 minutes **Cook:** 6 hours (low) + 30 minutes (high) or 3 hours (high)
Slow cooker size: 3½- or 4-quart

- **1 pound ground beef**
- **1 cup chopped onion (1 large)**
- **3 cloves garlic, minced**
- **1 14-ounce can beef broth**
- **3 cups frozen mixed vegetables**
- **1 14.5-ounce can diced tomatoes, undrained**
- **3 tablespoons tomato paste**
- **1 teaspoon dried oregano, crushed**
- **⅛ teaspoon ground cinnamon**
- **⅛ teaspoon ground nutmeg**
- **2 cups dried medium shell macaroni**
- **1 cup shredded Monterey Jack or crumbled feta cheese (4 ounces)**

1. In a large skillet, cook ground beef, onion, and garlic over medium heat until meat is brown and onion is tender. Drain off fat. Place in a 3½- or 4-quart slow cooker. Stir in broth, mixed vegetables, undrained tomatoes, tomato paste, oregano, cinnamon, and nutmeg.

2. Cover and cook on low-heat setting for 6 to 8 hours or on high-heat setting for 3 to 4 hours. If using low-heat setting, turn to high-heat setting. Add pasta. Cover and cook about 30 minutes more or until pasta is tender. Top each serving with cheese. Makes 6 servings.

Per serving: 446 cal., 16 g fat (7 g sat. fat), 64 mg chol., 539 mg sodium, 46 g carbo., 5 g fiber, 28 g pro.

Saucy Cheeseburger Sandwiches

Prep: 20 minutes
Cook: 6 hours (low) or 3 hours (high)
Slow cooker size: 3½- to 4-quart

- **2½ pounds lean ground beef**
- **1 10.75-ounce can condensed tomato soup**
- **1 cup finely chopped onion (2 medium)**
- **2 tablespoons tomato paste**
- **1 tablespoon Worcestershire sauce**
- **1 tablespoon yellow mustard**
- **2 teaspoons dried Italian seasoning, crushed**
- **2 cloves garlic, minced**
- **12 to 15 hamburger buns, split and toasted**
- **12 to 15 slices American cheese (9 to 12 ounces)**

1. In a large skillet, brown ground beef over medium heat. Drain off fat. Transfer meat to a 3½- or 4-quart slow cooker. Stir in soup, onion, ¼ cup *water*, the tomato paste, Worcestershire sauce, mustard, Italian seasoning, ¼ teaspoon *ground black pepper*, and the garlic.

2. Cover and cook on low-heat setting for 6 to 8 hours or on high-heat setting for 3 to 4 hours. Serve on hamburger buns topped with sliced cheese. Makes 12 to 15 servings.

Per serving: 382 cal., 17 g fat (8 g sat. fat), 80 mg chol., 734 mg sodium, 28 g carbo., 1 g fiber, 26 g pro.

French Dip with Mushrooms

Prep: 25 minutes **Cook:** 8 hours (low) or 4 hours (high) **Stand:** 10 minutes
Slow cooker size: 3½- to 6-quart

- 1 **3- to 3½-pound beef bottom round or rump roast**
- **Nonstick cooking spray**
- 4 **portobello mushrooms (3 to 4 inches in diameter)**
- 1 **14-ounce can beef broth seasoned with onion**
- 1 **large red onion, cut into ½-inch slices (optional)**
- 8 **hoagie buns, split and toasted**

1. Trim fat from meat. If necessary, cut roast to fit into a 3½- to 6-quart slow cooker. Lightly coat a large skillet with cooking spray; heat over medium heat. Brown meat on all sides in hot skillet. Place meat in the prepared cooker.

2. Clean mushrooms; remove and discard stems. Cut mushrooms into ¼-inch slices. Add to cooker. Pour broth over meat and mushrooms.

3. Cover and cook on low-heat setting for 8 to 9 hours or on high-heat setting for 4 to 4½ hours. Remove meat from cooker; cover and let stand for 10 minutes.

4. Meanwhile, using a slotted spoon, remove mushrooms; set aside. Thinly slice meat. Arrange meat, mushrooms, and, if desired, onion on toasted buns. Pour cooking juice into a measuring cup; skim off fat. Drizzle a little of the juice onto sandwiches; pour remaining juice into bowls for dipping. Makes 8 sandwiches.

Per sandwich: 646 cal., 17 g fat (4 g sat. fat), 98 mg chol., 970 mg sodium, 74 g carbo., 4 g fiber, 50 g pro.

Easy Cheesy Sloppy Joes

Prep: 25 minutes
Cook: 4½ hours (low) or 2 hours (high)
Slow cooker size: 3½- or 4-quart

- 3 pounds lean ground beef
- 1 cup chopped onion (1 large)
- 2 10¾-ounce cans condensed fiesta nacho cheese soup
- ¾ cup ketchup
- 18 hamburger or cocktail buns, split and toasted
- Pickles (optional)

1. In a 12-inch skillet or Dutch oven, cook ground beef and onion over medium heat until meat is browned and onion is tender. Drain off fat. In a 3½- or 4-quart slow cooker, combine meat mixture, soup, and ketchup.

2. Cover and cook on low-heat setting for 4½ hours or on high-heat setting for 2 hours. Serve meat mixture on toasted buns. If desired, garnish with pickles. Makes 18 servings.

Per serving: 288 cal., 11 g fat (4 g sat. fat), 50 mg chol., 563 mg sodium, 27 g carbo., 1 g fiber, 19 g pro.

Pesto Meatball Stew

Prep: 10 minutes
Cook: 5 hours (low) or 2½ hours (high)
Slow cooker size: 3½- or 4-quart

- 1 16-ounce package frozen cooked Italian-style meatballs (32), thawed
- 2 14½-ounce cans Italian-style stewed tomatoes, undrained
- 1 15- to 19-ounce can white kidney (cannellini) beans, rinsed and drained
- ¼ cup purchased basil pesto
- ½ cup finely shredded Parmesan cheese (2 ounces)

1. In a 3½- or 4-quart slow cooker, combine the meatballs, undrained tomatoes, drained beans, ½ cup *water*, and the pesto.
2. Cover and cook on low-heat setting for 5 to 7 hours or on high-heat setting for 2½ to 3½ hours. Ladle soup into bowls. Sprinkle with Parmesan cheese. Makes about 7 cups.

Per 1 cup: 408 cal., 27 g fat (10 g sat. fat), 34 mg chol., 1,201 mg sodium, 24 g carbo., 6 g fiber, 17 g pro.

Beefy Minestrone

Prep: 20 minutes
Cook: 8 hours (low) or 4 hours (high)
Slow cooker size: 3½- to 5-quart

- 1 pound lean ground beef
- 1 14-ounce can reduced-sodium beef broth
- 1¼ cups water
- 1 10-ounce package frozen mixed vegetables
- 1 14.5-ounce can whole peeled tomatoes, undrained, cut up
- 1 10.75-ounce can reduced-sodium and reduced-fat condensed tomato soup
- 1 tablespoon dried minced onion
- 1 teaspoon dried Italian seasoning, crushed
- ¼ teaspoon garlic powder

1. In a large skillet, cook beef until brown. Drain off fat. Transfer meat to a 3½- to 5-quart slow cooker. Stir in broth, water, vegetables, tomatoes, tomato soup, dried onion, Italian seasoning, and garlic powder.
2. Cover and cook on low-heat setting for 8 to 10 hours or on high-heat setting for 4 to 5 hours. If desired, top each serving with *crackers*. Makes 4 to 6 servings.

Per serving: 346 cal., 15 g total fat (6 g sat. fat), 71 mg chol., 684 mg sodium, 26 g carbo., 4.5 g fiber, 27 g pro.

Slow Cooker Chili

This easy chili gets its zesty flavor from salsa.

Prep: 25 minutes

Cook: 10 hours (low) or 5 hours (high)

Slow cooker size: 4- or 5-quart

- 1½ **pounds ground beef**
- 2 **15-ounce cans red kidney beans or small red beans, rinsed and drained**
- 2 **14.5-ounce cans Mexican-style stewed tomatoes, undrained**
- 1 **16-ounce jar salsa**
- ¾ **cup chopped onion (1 large)**
- ¾ **cup chopped green sweet pepper (1 medium)**
- 1 **clove garlic, minced**
- **Desired toppers, such as sliced green onion, corn chips, chopped tomato, and/or shredded cheddar cheese**

1. In a large skillet, brown ground beef over medium heat. Drain off fat. Transfer meat to a 4- or 5-quart slow cooker. Add drained beans, undrained tomatoes, salsa, onion, sweet pepper, and garlic to beef in cooker; stir to combine.

2. Cover and cook on low-heat setting for 10 to 12 hours or on high-heat setting for 5 to 6 hours. Serve chili with desired toppers. Makes 6 servings.

Per serving: 496 cal., 26 g fat (10 g sat. fat), 74 mg chol., 1,270 mg sodium, 40 g carbo., 10 g fiber, 32 g pro.

Taco Chili

Prep: 20 minutes
Cook: 4 hours (low) or 2 hours (high)
Slow cooker size: $3\frac{1}{2}$- or 4-quart

- 1 pound lean ground beef
- 2 15-ounce cans seasoned tomato sauce with diced tomatoes
- 1 15-ounce can chili beans with chili gravy
- 1 15-ounce can hominy or whole kernel corn, undrained
- 1 1.25-ounce envelope taco seasoning mix
- Dairy sour cream (optional)
- Shredded cheddar cheese (optional)

1. In a large skillet, brown ground beef over medium heat. Drain off fat.
2. In a $3\frac{1}{2}$- or 4-quart slow cooker, combine the meat, tomato sauce, beans with chili gravy, undrained hominy, and taco seasoning mix.
3. Cover and cook on low-heat setting for 4 to 6 hours or on high-heat setting for 2 to 3 hours. If desired, top each serving with sour cream and cheddar cheese. Makes 8 cups.

Per $1\frac{1}{2}$ cups: 477 cal., 18 g fat (6 g sat. fat), 71 mg chol., 1,998 mg sodium, 49 g carbo., 12 g fiber, 35 g pro.

Spaghetti Sauce with Italian Sausage

Prep: 15 minutes
Cook: 8 hours (low) or 4 hours (high)
Slow cooker size: 3½- or 4-quart

- ½ pound bulk Italian sausage
- ¼ pound lean ground beef
- ½ cup chopped onion
- 1 clove garlic, minced
- 1 14.5-ounce can diced tomatoes, undrained
- 1 8-ounce can reduced-sodium tomato sauce
- 1 4-ounce can sliced mushrooms, drained
- ½ cup chopped green sweet pepper (1 small)
- 2 tablespoons quick-cooking tapioca
- 1 bay leaf
- 1 teaspoon dried Italian seasoning, crushed
- ⅛ teaspoon ground black pepper
- dash salt
- hot cooked spaghetti
- fresh oregano (optional)

1. In a large skillet, brown sausage, ground beef, onion, and garlic over medium heat until onion is tender. Drain off fat.

2. In a 3½- or 4-quart slow cooker, stir together undrained tomatoes, tomato sauce, drained mushrooms, sweet pepper, tapioca, bay leaf, Italian seasoning, black pepper, and a dash salt. Stir in meat mixture. Cover and cook on low heat setting for 8 to 10 hours or on high heat setting for 4 to 5 hours. Discard bay leaf. Serve sauce over hot cooked spaghetti. If desired, sprinkle with *fresh oregano*. Makes 4 or 5 servings.

Per serving: 481 cal., 24 g total fat (9 g sat. fat), 79 mg chol., 788 mg sodium, 40 g carbo., 5 g fiber, 25 g pro.

Cuban Pork Sandwich

Prep: 30 minutes
Cook: 10 hours (low) or 5 hours (high)
Stand: 15 minutes
Slow cooker size: 3½- or 4-quart

- **1 3- to 3½-pound boneless pork shoulder roast**
- **¾ cup reduced-sodium chicken broth**
- **1 medium onion, cut into wedges**
- **1 cup packed cilantro leaves (1 bunch)**
- **2 tablespoons vinegar**
- **4 cloves garlic, minced**
- **1 teaspoon salt**
- **1 teaspoon ground cumin**
- **1 teaspoon dried oregano, crushed**
- **¼ teaspoon ground black pepper**
- **2 red onions, thinly sliced**
- **1 tablespoon cooking oil**
- **¼ cup lime juice**
- **8 ciabatta or French rolls, split**

1. Trim fat from roast; set aside. In a 3½- or 4-quart slow cooker, stir together broth, onion wedges, cilantro, ¼ cup *water*, vinegar, garlic, salt, cumin, oregano, and pepper. Add meat to slow cooker; spoon mixture over meat. Cover and cook on low-heat setting for 10 to 12 hours or on high-heat setting for 5 to 6 hours.

2. Just before serving, in a skillet, cook red onion in hot oil over medium-high heat until tender but not brown. Carefully add lime juice. Cook and stir until lime juice is evaporated.

3. Transfer meat to a cutting board; cool meat slightly. Using two forks, shred meat; discard fat. Serve meat and red onions on rolls. Makes 8 servings.

Per serving: 381 cal., 13 g fat (4 g sat. fat), 110 mg chol., 721 mg sodium, 25 g carbo., 2 g fiber, 38 g pro.

Pork Chops O'Brien

Prep: 20 minutes
Cook: 7 hours (low) or 3½ hours (high)
Slow cooker size: 3½- or 4-quart

- 5 **cups loose-pack frozen diced hash brown potatoes with onion and peppers, thawed**
- 1 **10.75-ounce can reduced-fat and reduced-sodium condensed cream of mushroom soup**
- ½ **cup bottled roasted red sweet peppers, drained and chopped**
- ½ **cup dairy sour cream**
- ½ **cup shredded Colby and Monterey Jack cheese (2 ounces)**
- ¼ **teaspoon ground black pepper**
- 4 **pork loin chops, cut ¾ inch thick**
- 1 **tablespoon cooking oil**
- 1 **2.8-ounce can french-fried onions**

1. Stir together thawed hash brown potatoes, soup, roasted sweet pepper, sour cream, cheese, and ground black pepper. Transfer mixture to 3½- or 4-quart slow cooker.
2. Trim fat from chops. In a skillet, brown chops in hot oil over medium heat; drain fat. Place chops on hash brown mixture in cooker.
3. Cover and cook on low-heat setting for 7 to 9 hours or on high-heat setting for 3½ to 4½ hours. Sprinkle each serving with french-fried onions. Makes 4 servings.

Per serving: 670 cal., 29 g fat (9 g sat. fat), 92 mg chol., 639 mg sodium, 64 g carbo., 4 g fiber, 37 g pro.

Cajun Pork

Prep: 20 minutes **Cook:** 7 hours (low) + 30 minutes (high) or 4 hours (high)
Slow cooker size: 3½- or 4-quart

- **Nonstick cooking spray**
- 2½ **to 3 pounds boneless pork shoulder, trimmed and cut into 1-inch cubes**
- 2 **medium yellow sweet peppers, cut into 1-inch pieces**
- 1 **tablespoon Cajun seasoning**
- 1 **14½-ounce can diced tomatoes with green pepper and onion, undrained**
- 1 **16-ounce package frozen cut okra**
- 1 **6-ounce package quick-cooking brown rice, cooked according to package directions**
- **Bottled hot pepper sauce (optional)**

1. Lightly coat a large skillet with nonstick cooking spray. Heat over medium heat. In hot skillet, cook meat, half at a time, until browned; drain off fat.
2. In a 3½- or 4-quart slow cooker, place meat and sweet pepper. Sprinkle with Cajun seasoning. Top with undrained tomatoes. Cover; cook on low-heat setting for 7 to 8 hours or on high-heat setting for 3½ to 4 hours.
3. If using low-heat setting, turn to high-heat setting. Stir in frozen okra. Cover and cook 30 minutes more. Serve over rice. If desired, pass hot pepper sauce. Makes 6 to 8 servings.

Per serving: 233 cal., 8 g fat (3 g sat. fat), 77 mg chol., 444 mg sodium, 15 g carbo., 4 g fiber, 25 g pro.

Shredded Pork Tacos

Prep: 30 minutes
Cook: 8 hours (low) or 4 hours (high)
Slow cooker size: 3½- or 4-quart

- 1 **2½- to 3-pound boneless pork shoulder roast**
- 1 **cup chicken broth**
- ½ **cup enchilada sauce or bottled salsa**
- 4 **8-inch soft flour tortillas or taco shells**
- **Assorted toppers, such as shredded lettuce, finely shredded Mexican-blend cheese, chopped tomato, sliced pitted ripe olives, and/or chopped avocado**
- **Dairy sour cream (optional)**

1. Trim fat from pork. If necessary, cut pork to fit in a 3½- or 4-quart slow cooker. Place pork in cooker. Add broth. Cover; cook on low-heat setting for 8 to 10 hours or on high-heat setting for 4 to 5 hours. Remove meat from cooker; discard broth. Using two forks, shred meat, discarding any fat. Reserve 2 cups of the meat. (Place remaining meat in an airtight container for another use; refrigerate up to 3 days or freeze up to 3 months.)

2. In a medium saucepan, combine reserved 2 cups meat and the enchilada sauce. Cover and cook over medium-low heat about 10 minutes or until heated through, stirring occasionally. Meanwhile, warm flour tortillas according to package directions.

3. To assemble tacos, place pork mixture in center of warm tortillas or in taco shells. Top as desired with lettuce, cheese, tomato, olives, and/or avocado. If desired, serve with sour cream. Makes 4 servings.

Per serving: 616 cal., 31 g fat (10 g sat. fat), 202 mg chol., 846 mg sodium, 20 g carbo., 3 g fiber, 61 g pro.

White & Green Chili

Prep: 20 minutes
Cook: 7 hours (low) or 3½ hours (high)
Slow cooker size: 3½- or 4-quart

- 1½ **pounds lean ground pork**
- 1 **cup chopped onion**
- 2 **15-ounce cans Great Northern beans, rinsed and drained**
- 1 **16-ounce jar green salsa**
- 1 **14-ounce can chicken broth**
- 1½ **teaspoons ground cumin**
- 2 **tablespoons snipped fresh cilantro**
- ⅓ **cup dairy sour cream (optional)**
- **Fresh cilantro sprigs (optional)**

1. In a large skillet, cook ground pork and onion over medium heat until meat is brown and onion is tender. Drain off fat. Transfer meat mixture to a 3½- or 4-quart slow cooker. Stir in drained beans, salsa, broth, and cumin.

2. Cover and cook on low-heat setting for 7 to 8 hours or on high-heat setting for 3½ to 4 hours.

3. Stir in the snipped cilantro. If desired, top each serving with sour cream and garnish with a cilantro sprig. Makes 6 servings.

Per serving: 348 cal., 9 g fat (4 g sat. fat), 53 mg chol., 613 mg sodium, 39 g carbo., 9 g fiber, 26 g pro.

Ribs & Kraut

Prep: 20 minutes
Cook: 7 hours (low) or 3½ hours (high)
Slow cooker size: 4- or 4½-quart

- **1 14-ounce can sauerkraut, drained**
- **1 large sweet onion, sliced (2 cups)**
- **2 medium tart cooking apples, peeled, cored, and sliced (about 2 cups)**
- **2 pounds boneless pork country-style ribs**
- **1 cup apple juice**
- **Snipped fresh chives**

1. In a 4- or 4½-quart slow cooker, place sauerkraut, onion, and apple. Top with pork. Pour apple juice over all.

2. Cover and cook on low-heat setting for 7 to 8 hours or on high-heat setting for 3½ to 4 hours. Serve with a slotted spoon. Sprinkle with chives. Makes 6 to 8 servings.

Per serving: 312 cal., 12 g fat (4 g sat. fat), 96 mg chol., 541 mg sodium, 19 g carbo., 4 g fiber, 30 g pro.

Orange Sesame Ribs

Prep: 15 minutes
Cook: 8 hours (low) or 4 hours (high)
Slow cooker size: 3½- or 4-quart

- **2½ to 3 pounds boneless country-style pork ribs**
- **Nonstick cooking spray**
- **1 10-ounce jar orange marmalade**
- **1 7¼-ounce jar hoisin sauce**
- **3 cloves garlic, minced**
- **1 teaspoon toasted sesame oil**

1. Trim fat from ribs. Lightly coat a large skillet with cooking spray; heat over medium heat. In hot skillet, brown ribs on all sides. Drain off fat. Place ribs in a 3½- or 4-quart slow cooker.

2. In a medium bowl, stir together marmalade, hoisin sauce, garlic, and sesame oil. Pour over ribs in cooker; stir to coat meat with sauce.

3. Cover and cook on low-heat setting for 8 to 10 hours or on high-heat setting for 4 to 5 hours. Transfer meat to a serving platter. Skim fat from sauce. Spoon some sauce over the meat. Pass remaining sauce. Makes 4 servings.

Per serving: 532 cal., 16 g fat (5 g sat. fat), 101 mg chol., 696 mg sodium, 66 g carbo., 0 g fiber, 33 g pro.

Cajun Shrimp & Rice

Prep: 20 minutes **Cook:** 5 hours (low) or 3 hours (high) + 15 minutes (high)
Slow cooker size: 3½- or 4-quart

- **2** **14.5-ounce cans diced tomatoes, undrained**
- **1** **14-ounce can reduced-sodium chicken broth**
- **1** **cup chopped onion (1 large)**
- **1** **cup chopped green sweet pepper (1 large)**
- **1** **6-ounce package long grain and wild rice mix**
- **¼** **cup water**
- **½** **teaspoon Cajun seasoning**
- **2** **cloves garlic, minced**
- **1** **pound cooked, peeled, and deveined shrimp**
- **Bottled hot pepper sauce (optional)**

1. In a 3½- or 4-quart slow cooker, stir together undrained tomatoes, chicken broth, onion, sweet pepper, rice mix (including seasoning packet), water, Cajun seasoning, and garlic.

2. Cover and cook on low-heat setting 5 to 6 hours or on high-heat setting 3 to 3½ hours. If using low-heat setting, turn to high-heat setting. Stir in shrimp. Cover and cook 15 minutes more. If desired, serve with hot pepper sauce. Makes 6 servings.

Per serving: 219 cal., 1 g total fat (0 g sat. fat), 148 mg chol., 1,001 mg sodium, 32 g carbo., 4 g fiber, 21 g pro.

Cheesy Mexican-Style Vegetable Soup

Prep: 15 minutes
Cook: 6 hours (low) or 3 hours (high)
Slow cooker size: 3½- or 4-quart

- 2 cups chopped zucchini
- 1 medium red sweet pepper, chopped
- 1 medium onion, chopped
- 1 15-ounce can black beans, rinsed and drained
- 1 10-ounce package frozen whole kernel corn, thawed
- 1 14.5-ounce can diced tomatoes with green chiles, undrained
- 1 16-ounce jar cheddar cheese pasta sauce
- 1 cup reduced-sodium chicken broth or vegetable broth
- Coarsely crushed tortilla chips and sliced fresh jalapeño pepper (optional)

1. In a 3½- or 4-quart slow cooker, place zucchini, sweet pepper, onion, drained beans, and corn. Pour undrained tomatoes over vegetables and beans. Combine cheese sauce and broth; pour over all.
2. Cover and cook on low-heat setting for 6 to 8 hours or on high-heat setting for 3 to 4 hours. Ladle soup into bowls and, if desired, top with crushed tortilla chips and jalapeño slices. Makes 5 to 6 servings.

Per serving: 289 cal., 14 g fat (5 g sat. fat), 35 mg chol., 1,381 mg sodium, 36 g carbo., 7 g fiber, 12 g pro.

Barley Vegetable Soup

Prep: 25 minutes
Cook: 8 hours (low) or 4 hours (high)
Slow cooker size: 3½- to 5-quart

- 1 15-ounce can red beans, rinsed and drained
- 1 10-ounce package frozen whole kernel corn
- ½ cup medium pearl barley
- 1 14½-ounce can no-salt stewed tomatoes, undrained
- 2 cups sliced fresh mushrooms
- 1 cup chopped onion (2 medium)
- ½ cup coarsely chopped carrot (1 medium)
- ½ cup coarsely chopped celery (1 stalk)
- 3 cloves garlic, minced
- 2 teaspoons dried Italian seasoning, crushed
- ¼ teaspoon ground black pepper
- 5 cups reduced-sodium vegetable broth or chicken broth

1. In a 3½- to 5-quart slow cooker, place drained beans, corn, barley, undrained tomatoes, mushrooms, onion, carrot, celery, garlic, Italian seasoning, and pepper. Pour broth over the top.
2. Cover and cook on low-heat setting for 8 to 10 hours or on high-heat setting for 4 to 5 hours. Makes 6 servings.

Per serving: 216 cal., 1 g total fat, 0 mg chol., 797 mg sodium, 15 g carbo., 9.5 g fiber, 11 g pro.

recipe index

Q

R

S

Metric Information

The charts on this page provide a guide for converting measurements from the U.S. customary system, used throughout this book, to the metric system.

Product Differences

Most of the ingredients called for in the recipes in this book are available in most countries. However, some are known by different names. Here are some common American ingredients and their possible counterparts:

Sugar (white) is granulated, fine granulated, or castor sugar.

Powdered sugar is icing sugar.

All-purpose flour is enriched, bleached or unbleached white household flour. When self-rising flour is used in place of all-purpose flour in a recipe that calls for leavening, omit the leavening agent (baking soda or baking powder) and salt.

Light-colored corn syrup is golden syrup.

Cornstarch is cornflour.

Baking soda is bicarbonate of soda.

Vanilla or vanilla extract is vanilla essence.

Bell peppers are capsicums.

Golden raisins are sultanas.

Volume & Weight

The United States traditionally uses cup measures for liquid and solid ingredients. The chart below shows the approximate imperial and metric equivalents. If you are accustomed to weighing solid ingredients, the following approximate equivalents will be helpful.

1 cup butter, castor sugar, or rice = 8 ounces = 1/2 pound = 250 grams

1 cup flour = 4 ounces = 1/4 pound = 125 grams

1 cup icing sugar = 5 ounces = 150 grams

Canadian and U.S. volume for a cup measure is 8 fluid ounces (237 ml), but the standard metric equivalent is 250 ml.

1 British imperial cup is 10 fluid ounces.

In Australia, 1 tablespoon equals 20 ml, and there are 4 teaspoons in the Australian tablespoon.

Spoon measures are used for smaller amounts of ingredients. Although the size of the tablespoon varies slightly in different countries, for practical purposes and for recipes in this book, a straight substitution is all that's necessary. Measurements made using cups or spoons should be level unless stated otherwise.

Common Weight Range Replacements

Imperial / U.S.	Metric
1/2 ounce	15 g
1 ounce	25 g or 30 g
4 ounces (1/4 pound)	115 g or 125 g
8 ounces (1/2 pound)	225 g or 250 g
16 ounces (1 pound)	450 g or 500 g
1 1/4 pounds	625 g
1 1/2 pounds	750 g
2 pounds or 2 1/4 pounds	1,000 g or 1 Kg

Oven Temperature Equivalents

Fahrenheit Setting	Celsius Setting*	Gas Setting
300°F	150°C	Gas Mark 2 (very low)
325°F	160°C	Gas Mark 3 (low)
350°F	180°C	Gas Mark 4 (moderate)
375°F	190°C	Gas Mark 5 (moderate)
400°F	200°C	Gas Mark 6 (hot)
425°F	220°C	Gas Mark 7 (hot)
450°F	230°C	Gas Mark 8 (very hot)
475°F	240°C	Gas Mark 9 (very hot)
500°F	260°C	Gas Mark 10 (extremely hot)
Broil	Broil	Grill

*Electric and gas ovens may be calibrated using celsius. However, for an electric oven, increase celsius setting 10 to 20 degrees when cooking above 160°C. For convection or forced air ovens (gas or electric), lower the temperature setting 25°F/10°C when cooking at all heat levels.

Baking Pan Sizes

Imperial / U.S.	Metric
9x1 1/2-inch round cake pan	22- or 23x4-cm (1.5 L)
9x1 1/2-inch pie plate	22- or 23x4-cm (1 L)
8x8x2-inch square cake pan	20x5-cm (2 L)
9x9x2-inch square cake pan	22- or 23x4.5-cm (2.5 L)
11x7x1 1/2-inch baking pan	28x17x4-cm (2 L)
2-quart rectangular baking pan	30x19x4.5-cm (3 L)
13x9x2-inch baking pan	34x22x4.5-cm (3.5 L)
15x10x1-inch jelly roll pan	40x25x2-cm
9x5x3-inch loaf pan	23x13x8-cm (2 L)
2-quart casserole	2 L

U.S. / Standard Metric Equivalents

1/8 teaspoon = 0.5 ml
1/4 teaspoon = 1 ml
1/2 teaspoon = 2 ml
1 teaspoon = 5 ml
1 tablespoon = 15 ml
2 tablespoons = 25 ml
1/4 cup = 2 fluid ounces = 50 ml
1/3 cup = 3 fluid ounces = 75 ml
1/2 cup = 4 fluid ounces = 125 ml
2/3 cup = 5 fluid ounces = 150 ml
3/4 cup = 6 fluid ounces = 175 ml
1 cup = 8 fluid ounces = 250 ml
2 cups = 1 pint = 500 ml
1 quart = 1 litre